FIRST HIRED, LAST FIRED

HOW TO MAKE YOURSELF INDISPENSABLE IN AN AGE OF DOWNSIZING, MERGERS, AND RESTRUCTURING

ROBERT M. BRAMSON, PH.D., AND SUSAN J. BRAMSON

CONTEMPORARY BOOKS

Library of Congress Cataloging-in-Publication Data

Bramson, Robert M.
    First hired, last fired : how to make yourself indispensable in an
age of downsizing, mergers, and restructuring / Robert M. Bramson.
        p.   cm.
    ISBN 0-8092-3130-1
    1. Employee motivation.   2. Commitment (Psychology)
3. Employees—Rating of.   4. Downsizing of organizations.
I. Bramson, Susan J. 1940– .   II. Title.
HF5549.5.M63B72   1999
658.14—dc21   98-45610
                                                                      CIP

Notes on usage: To assure privacy, we have changed the names of
the interviewees, the indispensable people they described, and, in a
few cases, the nature of the organizations in which they were
employed. We also edited some quotations for clarity, to eliminate the
repetition and backtracking normally found in informal speech, or to
simplify sentence structure. Where the narrative seemed to work better
with a singular pronoun, we have tried to alternate between *she* and *he*
rather than use the awkward *he or she*. After all, gender does not
determine either indispensability or its lack.

Interior design by Scott Rattray

Published by Contemporary Books
A division of NTC/Contemporary Publishing Group, Inc.
4255 West Touhy Avenue, Lincolnwood (Chicago), Illinois 60646-1975 U.S.A.
Copyright © 1999 by Control Resources Development Corp.
Printed in the United States of America
International Standard Book Number: 0-8092-3130-1
99 00 01 02 03 04 LB 18 17 16 15 14 13 12 11 10 9 8 7 6 5 4 3 2 1

To FRED BATKIN JR., rancher,
community leader, public servant;
who taught me much about the
old, indispensable virtues
—R.M.B.

To BOB BRAMSON, my partner,
lover, friend, and mentor—who
taught me to believe in myself
and reach for the impossible
—S.J.B.

Contents

Acknowledgments vii

SECTION I
WHAT INDISPENSABLE PEOPLE ARE LIKE 1

1 Introduction 3

2 Certain Qualities of Mind 15

3 Personal Characteristics of
Indispensable People 27

SECTION II
BECOMING AN INDISPENSABLE PERSON 73

4 Creating an Indispensable-Person
Role for Yourself 75

5 Planning Your Indispensability Program 95

SECTION III
POINTERS FOR BUILDING YOUR REPERTOIRE
OF INDISPENSABLE ATTRIBUTES 119

6 Thinking Like an Indispensable Person 123

7 Enhancing Your IP Interpersonal Skills 159

8 Developing an IP Perspective 219

References 245

Acknowledgments

I AM INDEBTED to many for the substance of this book and for the encouragement to follow up a vague inkling with research and writing.

First and foremost, my thanks to every one of those willing and supportive people who assented to a lengthy interview in the midst of a too-busy life. They provided most of the content of Chapters 1 to 3.

Of the many writers on organizational lore not directly cited, several deserve special mention. Stuart Atkins, Allan Katcher, and the late Elias Porter Jr. first called my attention to the strength-weakness irony, to use their term, that keeps even the most indispensable of us from attaining true perfection of character. The work of C. West Churchman prompted me (along with my co-researchers, Allen F. Harrison, Nicholas Parlette, and Susan Bramson) to explore managerial thinking styles.

My consulting partners, Lucy Gill and Susan Bramson (to whom I am also happily espoused), have taught me new perspectives on the interpersonal aspects of work life. They have also added much to my store of practical ploys for helping our clients be the best they can.

Several individuals were particularly helpful in the formative stages of this project: Jeremy Bramson (who contributed the present title); Wendy Waits; Eric Welch, vice president of Innosys Corporation; Captain Patrick Gallaher, USMC; and Frank Jirik, senior executive vice president of the San Jose Sharks hockey organization.

I extend a heartfelt thank-you to Debra Kalmon for transcribing the first draft of this book and helping to keep it on schedule.

My children and their families provided encouragement and enthusiasm, as they have in the past. I hope they know how much I appreciate their support.

Many thanks to Carol Mann, my friend and agent, who was—as usual—always there, and to my Contemporary Books editor, Kara Leverte. When doubts crept in, they both insisted that this book would provide something uniquely helpful. I now believe they were right.

ROBERT M. BRAMSON

WHEN BOB DIED on September 7, 1998, I was relieved that this manuscript had been delivered the previous week, and I knew the task of final copyediting remained to be done. My special thanks go to my friend, and Bob's partner, Lucy Gill, for crying, laughing, and editing with me. Your knowledge and skill as an author and fellow consultant brought closure to this monumental task. Also, I want to thank my daughter-in-law Kathleen Gallaher. Your thoughts, clarity, and humor were essential to completing this job.

I'd like to give special thanks to our agent, Carol Mann, for supporting me and encouraging me to finish the task Bob had begun, and to Kara Leverte, our editor, for smoothing the way to meeting deadlines.

My friends Pat Meyer and Sally Lund receive my undying gratitude. You kept asking me what I needed, then listened to me fuss, cry, and despair over the task of ever completing the editing. You kept telling me I didn't have to do it alone, and you were right.

The Greeley Hill Rowdy Bunch kept me grounded and nurtured me through the early months of grieving the loss of my co-author, my partner, and my spouse. Words can't begin to tell you how much your support and laughter kept me going. Thank you.

To *all* of my children, thank you for loving and supporting me as we grieved Dad's passing together.

I thank my mom, Carolyn Batkin; you are the one who has given me continuous encouragement with your zest for life and adventure.

And lastly, thank you Bob for sharing your warmth, humor, love, and everlasting confidence in me to accomplish what often seemed impossible.

SUSAN J. BRAMSON

What Indispensable People Are Like

CAN AN EMPLOYEE really be indispensable? Common wisdom holds that no one is. However, our research shows that many managers say they have an employee they would keep at almost any cost—someone who would be the last to go, even if the company had to lay off everyone else. In today's uncertain business climate, where many have fallen victim to mergers, restructuring, and downsizing, it makes sense to be that kind of employee.

To show you how, we start with a description of indispensable employees. The three chapters in Section 1 tell you what kind of person to be if you want to be viewed as indispensable. Chapter 1 introduces what we mean by "indispensable" and explains how we drew our conclusions. Chapters 2 and 3 describe the characteristics of indispensability identified from our interview tapes and notes. Chapter 2 focuses on the qualities that make indispensable people good problem solvers. Chapter 3 details the other personal characteristics of these valued employees.

Introduction

ECONOMY EXPANDING, economy contracting, or economy coasting along, the orgy of mergers, acquisitions, restructuring, budget cuts, and downsizing continues unabated. Whether this propensity for drastic action is a rational response to a rambunctious global marketplace or simply an easy way for CEOs to justify (and cash in on) their generous stock options by pulling off something really *big*, such organizational transformations are with us for the foreseeable future. Whatever else they may do, one invariable result is major disruption for employees at every level, including the loss of whatever shreds of job security were left over from the old days of lifelong corporate and government careers. Caught up in this uncertain era, we have only one defense: to make ourselves so indispensable that any organization would be foolish to let us go—and that we'll know we are so employable that we won't care whether or not they do.

This book is about how to make yourself virtually layoff-proof. It tells you about the qualities that moved the bosses and coworkers of over sixty diverse employees to call them virtually indispensable. We'll also tell which qualities, though often cited as essential, are irrelevant to being placed in that select group. Most importantly, this book tells you how to become indispensable at work if you want or need to.

The characteristics that make some people seem indispensable (we'll refer to those indispensable people as IPs) have been distilled from interviews with nearly fifty of their managers and coworkers, and from twenty-seven years of observing these irreplaceable people at work. In later chapters you'll find concrete suggestions on how to acquire the specific skills that mark one as indispensable.

Actually, you may almost be there anyway and just don't know it, or perhaps you haven't thought about how to show it. If so, you'll benefit from knowing more about what makes an employee *seem* indispensable to those who count. Or you may be one of those ambitious people who have industriously developed the skills that they thought would fit them for positions of trust and power. If so, your problem may be that you haven't really known what the differentiating qualities are. You repaired faults that don't seem to matter much; you acquired skills that—while useful enough—don't mark you as special. (The reciprocal of this is also true: management frequently promotes people whose particular attributes can't produce the desired richness of performance.) Unfortunately, much of what appears in management journals and textbooks is based upon what academics or consultants *think* will be useful, derived from their notions of how organizations ought to work and their at-a-distance observations. One purpose of this book is to clarify just which employee characteristics do make a difference to the people who make personnel decisions.

In a larger sense, the characteristics of the select group of people you'll read about in the following chapters dramatically point up the qualities that workers at every level will need if the promise of organizational transformation found in current management literature is to be realized. The sobering lessons of the turbulent restructurings of the first half of the nineties are that teamwork, creativity, superb customer service, or a quality orientation do not come into being simply because management has reengineered, downsized, excised corporate layers, or mandated employee empowerment. The data we've gathered in preparing for this book clearly show that it is the meanings that employees invest in their roles, as well as the particular skills they have attained, that make the difference between performance that is good enough and that which is superb.

Is Anyone Really Indispensable?

Can anyone ever be said to be indispensable, that is, incapable of being set aside? After all, employees fall ill, take extensive vacations, resign, and eventually retire, yet their organizations continue to survive. True enough, but some employees *seem* so valuable that it becomes difficult to imagine how their organization could function well without them. In fact, that is precisely the description we gave our interviewees: "Think of those individuals of your acquaintance who have given such value to their part of the organization that no matter how drastic a cutback, they would be the very last to go." The practicality of this working definition of indispensability shows in the following example of what one manager said about such an employee:

> I can't really say that Matthew is truly indispensable; that is, if he were to quit tomorrow, our company wouldn't fold. But when you asked me who would be the very last person that we would ever let go, Matt immediately came to mind. I depend upon him to help me think things through, especially when there's a lot riding on the answer. He's a mainstay around the office, people look to him for answers, as I do, and he seems to be willing to help just about anyone. I don't mean that he's a pushover, and he's certainly not chatty. He doesn't let himself be leaned on, and some have gotten sore at him because he turned them off when they were asking for too much help. He can be abrupt sometimes. But it all adds up to Matt being as indispensable as anyone can be because of what he does and who he is.

Who and How Did We Interview?

In preparing for this book, we contacted fifty-one executives, managers, and supervisors from both white- and blue-collar organizations, large and small. Forty-five of those we solicited, from technology-based, manufacturing, marketing, sales, health care, agricultural, and governmental organizations, made themselves available for personal interviews. While most singled out a current or former subordinate, many also told about coworkers or present or previous bosses. In some cases, we were able to interview the IPS themselves.

The interviews were open-ended conversations and always began with our description of indispensability, followed by "What is it that they do or say that leads you to think of them as indispensable?" This method has the great advantage of avoiding a danger of a more structured survey approach: narrowing the range of behaviors that might be elicited. Surveys work well when you know what you are looking for and you just want to find out how much of it is there. But we were not at all sure that there were any common characteristics, much less what they would be. In addition, surveys lose the richness of information provided by a more informal open-ended approach.

Who Made Up Our Cadre of Indispensable People?

Our forty-five respondents described sixty-seven indispensable people, 56 percent of whom were male. In terms of occupation, 16 percent were blue-collar employees, all in supervisory or lead person positions; the balance worked in diverse technical, professional, or support positions ranging in level from staff assistant to executive. Their job titles ranged from mechanic and lift truck operator to corporate controller and chief executive officer. In age, as estimated by the interviewees who described them, the IPs ranged from twenty-seven to sixty-eight, the largest group clustering toward the older end of the distribution.

Although the particulars of their jobs obviously differed, the characteristics that made these people stand out as indispensable were quite the same regardless of sex, organizational level, or collar color. We asked the interviewees to estimate how common such indispensable people were. The estimates ranged from 1 out of 100 to 10 out of 100.

What Makes an Employee Seem Indispensable?

When we began our first round of interviews, we were unsure of whether we would get *any* responses other than "No!" However, most of those we contacted could name at least one highly valued person—sometimes several. Even more gratifying, they could describe in some detail just what it was that made them consider those people special. Here, as an example, is a somewhat abridged description of one of the early interviews:

> The only way I could arrange an interview with John Williams, vice president and co-owner of a successful software company, was to sit with him in his office while he munched his way through a sandwich lunch. Yes, he acknowledged after I had told him what we were after, he knew of an indispensable employee; in fact, she was

the one I had seen leaving his office just as I was coming in. I tried to remember what she looked like—thirtyish, rather rumpled, smiling a little as she held the door for me. Next to himself and his partners, John said, she would be the last to go if drastic layoffs were ever necessary.

"What makes Erica indispensable?" he said, after a pause. "Well, I can tell you what it's not. It's definitely not just technical competence that makes an employee indispensable, unless maybe you're talking about some kind of proven genius or supercreative person. Yes, you have to have a reasonable amount of know-how, but thankfully we have a lot of highly skilled people—at least three more technically knowledgeable about computers than she is. They're certainly important contributors, but even though it's hard to find people like that these days, they can be replaced, especially during a downturn, which is when we'd be into heavy layoffs. It's a little harder to pin down just what it is.

"You know, I've never really thought about her as being indispensable, but as soon as you asked if I knew someone like that, I thought of her. For one thing, probably the main thing, she has a very wide-ranging view of what this company is about. She's primarily a technical person, but she seems to understand the need for keeping an eye on the bottom line. I can give her a go-ahead on a project, knowing that she never forgets to balance the cost against the benefits. If she doesn't see a real payoff in a project she's working on or, for that matter, in anyone's project—even mine—she'll propose shelving it. On the other hand, she always seems to be thinking about what else can be done that will expand our range of products.

"How is she with people? Well, there are funny contrasts. She is rather a no-nonsense person, at times to the point of seeming brusque. She isn't much for small talk.

In fact, in groups she's mostly a listener unless she's making a point or talking up one of our products with a customer. On the other hand, people go to her a lot for advice—me included. The thing that really stands out about her is sort of a contradiction. When she's working on a problem, she'll listen to ideas from almost anyone, and she obviously takes them seriously. But when she's made a decision—to keep on with a product line that seems to be costing too much, to mention a recent example—she'll defend her plan against all comers, even my partner, who's the CEO. On the other hand, she can be tough like that without seeming to attack anybody's good sense or without sounding like a rebel.

"Does all this add up to indispensable?" John paused, staring at the remains of his lunch. "There's something more, but it's harder to pin down. Before I went into business with my two partners, I'd worked for a bunch of companies, and I think I was always a good employee. But when you have your heart and money invested in your own company, you see things differently. Erica doesn't have a dime in this company except, of course, her retirement, but she acts, talks, and sounds just like an owner."

Like John Williams, most of those we interviewed readily identified an indispensable employee, a boss, subordinate, or peer, and then struggled to articulate the qualities that made them so. Eventually, most were able to portray their own particular Ericas, some succinctly, others at exhaustive length. Although their indispensable people differed considerably in the details of their work lives, certain common characteristics consistently surfaced. Few were graced with every attribute; indispensable people are not simply paragons of every virtue. But they all had acquired a core of particular habits of mind, uncommon perspectives about work relationships and roles, and specific interpersonal skills that made them uniquely valued.

Throughout the balance of the book, *indispensable* will mean "even in a drastic cutback, the last to go." To place the qualities that mark a person as indispensable in perspective, let's examine some that don't. The following attributes, though often bandied about as earmarking the best employees, were considered by our interviewees to be, at the least, irrelevant to the question of indispensability:

- Being the most technically competent person around

- Simple dependability—for example, always showing up, completing assignments on time

- Working long hours and weekends

- Deciding quickly

- Appearing aggressively success-oriented

- Loyalty to the organization

- Being seen as highly creative

- A pleasing personality—charming, getting along well with everyone

You may have found some surprises here; we did. It's not that dependability isn't necessary, or that pleasant people aren't nice to have around; they are. But neither quality singles someone out as one of those "never want to lose them" people whom we're calling indispensable. Dependability is assumed in any pretty good employee, even though, as one interviewee put it, "It's not always there." If you don't usually meet your report deadlines, if you don't show up with reasonable regularity, you exclude yourself from consideration. But being dependable simply makes you one more of an acceptable crowd, any of whom can be let go when a crunch comes.

In broad brush, these are the qualities that *do* make indispensable people stand out as special:

- *Certain qualities of mind*—Indispensable people have a "systems" orientation to problem solving. They see beyond the surface of problems and don't oversimplify complex issues. They see connections that others miss. They have flexible minds. They get broad input and think a lot before they decide. They are loaded with practical intelligence (IQ tests don't measure it), an uncommon form of common sense.

- *An odd notion about "employment"*—IPs have an "owner's" mentality, even when they are not owners. They see themselves as responsible for the success of the whole enterprise. They feel more responsible to their own notions of quality and ethics than to the policies and dictates of their organizations, yet they are not rebels. Although their work is highly satisfying to them, they keep it in balance with other aspects of their lives.

- *Readiness to interact with others (but only in certain ways)*—IPs help when it's needed (but only then). They willingly work as part of a team (but only where teams are needed). They are supportive of coworkers (but only those who deserve support). They are candid (but not aggressively so). They listen thoughtfully to others (but stay with their own high standards).

- *Relative freedom from most organizational tensions and conflicts*—IPs are confident of their abilities but are continuous learners. They show little status consciousness, neither subservient to the high nor arrogant or patronizing to the low. They avoid turf battles. They are not driven to compete for higher levels of success, but are extraordinarily productive because they seek to better their own performance.

- *Positive, can-do attitude*—IPs are consistently positive, yet realistic, about the possibilities in any problem situation: "Something can always be done to move us forward."

- *Adaptability to change*—Everywhere we look, jobs, careers, even the nature of work all seem to be in flux. Yet, in our work with IPs, we have been struck by how well they adapt to this ubiquitous upheaval. They seem somehow untouched by the same shifts in policy, mood, and direction that so frustrate and depress most of their coworkers. Self-motivated, focused on how to use themselves to best tackle the tasks at hand, they remain confident that whatever the circumstance, they will be all right.

Based on years of experience in helping others to develop themselves to their real potential, we are convinced that nothing sets the stage for personal change more than clearly visualizing precisely how you would behave if you were the kind of person you want to be. As you read through the next two chapters, picture yourself imbued with the indispensable qualities you'll find described there. Are you already an almost indispensable person, needing only to identify the one or two particular skills you're short? Do you need only to find new ways to use your talents and abilities? Either way, create a picture of yourself as someone impossible to replace.

2

Certain Qualities
of Mind

As OUR INTERVIEWEES hesitatingly pieced out the story of what golden attributes made their indispensable people so singularly valuable, their first thoughts most often went to some version of "really good at solving problems." From one interview to the next, a cluster of distinctive qualities emerged, irrespective of the IPS' age, gender, organizational level, white- or blue-collar occupation, the nature of the work itself, or any other characteristic discernible to us. Indispensable people can see into problems, have a systems view, don't oversimplify, are thoughtful and reflective, can articulate complex ideas and relationships, gather broad input before they decide, and have remarkably flexible minds. (In describing indispensable qualities of mind for this chapter, we depended primarily on the accounts of interviewees, supplemented by observations of IPs and informed by the insights of various students of the practical applications of intelligence, as detailed in Diane F. Halpern's *Thought and Knowledge* and Robert J. Sternberg's *Intelligence Applied*.)

They Can See into Problems

Virtually all the interviewees said—often with a bit of awe—that the IPs they had in mind had, as one interviewee described it, "an ability to see *into* problems." The IPs themselves often thought of this ability as a knack for visualizing how the pieces of the problem they were working on were interconnected, a somewhat freestanding ability, not related to technical expertise or educational level. The characterizations that follow, each pertaining to a different IP, are extraordinarily similar:

> He's not the most knowledgeable—our guys are a pretty brainy bunch—but when we're faced with a really tough project and run into trouble, he can draw out the important elements from the whole thing. He seems to be able to make very complex issues seem simple—maybe *graspable* is a better word than *simple*.

> He's first-rate at putting his finger on what will fix the problem. It's not just getting all the facts together; he does enough of that, but so does everybody else. I think

that it's more having a feel for what depends upon what and where the fit isn't right. Am I making sense?

When I say that he can cut the mustard, what I mean is he seems to be able to go right to the core of the problem, to cut away everything that's extraneous, and to put his finger on what needs to be done.

She's good at cutting through, at getting to the nub.

An IP described the quality of "seeing from the inside" this way:

I have a very good ability to visualize. I'm not an engineer, but I can look at blueprints and visualize the process. Hackers have that ability; working in materials systems is the same thing.

They Have a Systems View

Indispensable people show an aptitude for seeing the interconnections among disparate events. That perspective, often called a systems view, reveals that a whole is more than the sum of its parts, every aspect of the world is somehow interconnected with every other aspect, and how well the interconnections work determines how effectively the system will operate. Such a view offers a considerable advantage because it widens your focus in all directions. For example, you will not be too much taken aback when your immediate concerns turn out to be the natural consequence of a seemingly innocuous decision made long ago.

The following comments show the flavor of this IP attribute:

I think of Eric as having a special kind of judgment in the way he thinks about things. It's not just intelligence—everyone here is bright—but it's being able to restructure situations in your mind. I don't exactly know how else to describe it. In a way, it's a kind of creative process, based on how the facts of the situation come together. For example, Eric sees chances to do more than what customers ask for. I don't mean just selling them an added option—he's not really a salesman—but seeing how what they want done might be done better in a different way. It's as if he sees more clearly than they do how our stuff is related to what they really need. The fascinating thing is that the customers, instead of feeling hassled or conned, get all excited about his proposal.

The other quality that made her so critical was she could see how things were related. Not just "the big picture" as an abstraction but the way all the different pieces of a job were connected in a crucial way, so that if you change one, it changes a lot more, in both good and bad ways. She's saved us from bad mistakes.

What makes him so special to me is that he can visualize and plan on many levels—day to day, several weeks, three months, three years, by unit, by squadron, by area—not losing sight of how it all fits together. In planning complex military operations, that ability is immensely valuable, but I've found that most people can't do that well, even though operations planning really requires it.

Yes, she has her areas of expertise, but the main thing is that she can see the big picture. Well, she's not alone in that; some can see the big picture, but they founder on the specifics. She can see how they both fit together. I think that's what helps her to set priorities that really mean something.

They Don't Oversimplify

H. L. Mencken once wrote, "For every problem, there is a neat, clean solution—it is always wrong." In his 1994 book, *Greatness*, Dean Keith Simonton elaborated on that bit of cryptic sarcasm by describing the difference between complex and simple thinkers: "Someone [who thinks] with high complexity can process multiple perspectives and then integrate them into a coherent viewpoint. In contrast, a person with low complexity can handle only a single perspective; he or she views the world in simplistic, black and white terms." Indispensable people are able to think complexly about the complicated issues that face them, and this quality is clearly recognized by bosses, peers, and subordinates. Here are some quotes that capture the essence of their capacity for complex thinking:

One thing that fascinates me about her way of approaching problems is that she seems to rotate the problem in her mind, looking at it from a bunch of viewpoints: How does it look to our customers? Is it an on-line manufacturing issue? If we do it this way, what will that do to engineering? More than that, she can switch mind-sets without losing her composure or the sight of what our original goal was. By the way, this makes her terrific at joint planning with other functions, and especially in negotiation where seeing the other guy's side is really important.

What stands out is his ability to see the marriage between technical and operations requirements.

There are, of course, both advantages and disadvantages to complex thinking. A variety of psychological researchers show that complex thinkers are far better at solving difficult or complicated problems than those whose thinking is more of the "it's either A or B" variety. Certainly most governmental and business decisions, rarely simple in either cause or effect, ought to be made by weighing a complex of positive and negative trade-offs, which may shift even as the decision is made. It seems self-evident that the more one can keep the totality of all these impinging factors in mind, the more realistic will be the actions decided upon.

On the other hand, as political leaders soon discover, most people are impatient with the full complexity of issues. After all, it is easier to drum up enthusiasm for solving problems defined in simple black-and-white terms. Shades of gray are never a dramatic attention getter.

They Are Thoughtful People

Indispensable people are thoughtful, reflective rather than rapid-fire decision makers. It is not that indispensable people are slow thinkers or that they can't come up with fast action when it's required. But when issues are complex, they take time to figure out, think through, and put together. One manager put it this way:

> You know, she does something strange: She thinks a lot—not blue sky but practically oriented thinking—about a problem before she starts moving. I've tried to learn to do that from her. What she says she's doing is getting a feel for the whole situation—kind of like walking through a maze.

They Can Articulate Complex Ideas and Relationships

Persistence—even pleasure—in untangling complexities is quite a different talent from the ability to explain to others how the pieces fit. Many of the indispensables in our sample, though not a majority, had a good measure of both. For those who had it, the ability to articulate complicated combinations of facts, events, and meanings stood out as particularly valuable.

> It's hard to say whether she sees the point better than I do or whether it's that she can describe it better. But one of her talents is really remarkable: After a long discussion and hours of poring over charts and data analyses, she will proceed to the flip chart and in ten sentences summarize the results of all our laborious thinking. After she's put some complex notion into words, I always feel as if "Sure, I knew that." But did I really?

What amazes me about Phil is that he is so good in front of our advisory groups. Some of our analyses and proposals are very data heavy, and many of the advisers haven't really done their homework. Phil will take them through the material, emphasizing the key points, and even more important, will get across the fundamental ideas so they understand them. It's a real gift. I wish I had more of it, and I wish more of our staff did. Some of our smartest guys are not very good at explaining their ideas to other people.

They Gather Broad Input Before Deciding

Although it might well be considered a group management skill, a penchant for gathering broad input prior to deciding was most often mentioned in relation to finding the right answers to complex problems. It's certainly not the first time a quality like this has been coupled with excellent performance. In a comparison of managers who were cited as having "the right stuff" with those who did not, Michael Lombardo of the Center for Creative Leadership pointed out that superior managers asked a wider range of sources for more information and advice. While IPs stick firmly with their convictions *after* they have reached a conclusion, they welcome all sorts of input before.

It's not difficult to see how attending to many divergent views flows naturally from a perspective that is broad-gauged and comfortable with complexity. A quote from a division chief in a large government bureaucracy captures this combination of attributes well:

Being somewhat of an old-fashioned manager, I was concerned when John joined us as head of an important new program. I was used to people who sat down with all the paperwork and came up with their own ideas about what the proper application of resources would be, the best scheduling of work orders, and so forth. Then there was John, who would call a meeting of everyone who might be involved, listen to all their ideas, and fill up a flip chart with half a dozen different ways to set up a project. My first thought was "Uh-oh, he's going to be a wishy-washy, always-changing-his-mind manager." I could not have been more wrong. He still gets more input than I think is really necessary, but once he has arrived at a decision, he goes right into action and will defend his plan even against the double thinking that often hits us from the corporate staff.

One habit that Charlie has that I wish my other guys would pick up is that when we get a new machine in, Charlie not only goes to training and reads all the paperwork, but he will get around to the operators—especially the ones who've been around—and ask them what problems he should expect—you know, the kind that are never in the manuals the engineers write but that skilled toolmakers pick up on.

They Are Adaptive Thinkers

Whatever else one can say about indispensable people, they are not rigid or inflexible. They can switch mind-sets quickly, take a fresh look when new facts, opinions, or interpretations come along, and recast pieces of a problem, testing each reformulation against some pragmatic standard such as "Will it move us forward enough to make it worthwhile?"

> He could switch from practical problem solving to concept and theory in a flash—at home designing something new or working out a problem with the blue-collars on the floor. They respected that he knew his stuff as an engineer, but he was also good with his hands—I mean professionally good, not amateur good.

> He could see beyond the immediate task. For instance, he'd ask, "Wouldn't one combined report show how things relate better than two separate ones?"

> He can switch mind-sets without losing his composure or losing sight of the original goal. Makes him terrific as a negotiator and in joint planning with other functions.

> Her greatest strength as head of our project was being able to go from meeting to meeting—with street people, with company CEOs, with law enforcement people, with college academics—and relate to them around what their main issues were. A tremendous flexibility of mind.

They Are More Objective

Bosses and peers frequently said IPs are relatively unbiased in their thinking, less influenced by tradition, by personal theories about how the world *should* work, by their individual past experiences, and even by their own self-interest. This greater objectivity may be a valuable by-product of a willingness to pay serious attention to differing perspectives.

IP Qualities and Intelligence

Do these "indispensable" qualities of mind simply reduce to high general intelligence? Is a high IQ all that's required to think like an indispensable person? The answer to the first question may be a qualified yes. Our indispensable people do seem to have a lot of what psychologist Robert Sternberg calls "practical intelligence," the kind of intelligence that enables one to deal effectively with the daily affairs of life. From time to time Sternberg and several associates have asked diverse groups of people to describe the qualities that they thought were characteristic of intelligent people. Here is a partial listing of the thinking behaviors that Sternberg and his colleagues said people called signs of "practical problem-solving ability":

- Reasons logically and well
- Identifies connections among ideas
- Sees all aspects of a problem
- Keeps an open mind
- Responds thoughtfully to others' ideas
- Sizes up situations well
- Gets to the heart of problems
- Goes to original sources for basic information

- Poses problems in an optimal way

- Is a good source of ideas

- Perceives implied assumptions and conclusions

- Listens to all sides of an argument

- Deals with problems resourcefully

Although Sternberg's list reports what ordinary people *thought* were the signs of practical intelligence and our interviewees were those who knew the indispensable people well, the two sets of attributes have obvious similarities. We often think of these qualities as "common sense," even though we know that possessing them to a high degree is quite uncommon. Uncommon enough that our interviewees attributed them just to the one out of ten employees considered indispensable.

So is practical intelligence what IQ tests measure? Probably not. As Sternberg and others have pointed out, high IQ scores, combined with other measures such as high school grades, do predict academic success reasonably well, but they are poor predictors of effectiveness on the job. Recall that interviewees seldom attributed the highest level of technical competence, a quality often associated with high IQ, to indispensable people. There is more to indispensability than a good measure of practical intelligence. In Chapter 3 we'll examine other personal qualities that enable IPs to use their good minds to the fullest extent.

3

Personal Characteristics of Indispensable People

A PENCHANT FOR thinking and a generous helping of practical intelligence are not the only attributes that distinguish indispensable people from their coworkers. To be sure, none of these other attributes are unique only to indispensable people. Any of them could be ascribed to most good yet not at all indispensable employees. Instead, indispensability results from the additive effect of these qualities and the way they intertwine. Consider, for example, Stuart Pickett, an indispensable middle manager, as he was described by the human resources director of a moderate-sized but rapidly growing manufacturer of high-tech medical equipment.

Actually, my first impression of Stuart was rather negative. I had been working with his predecessor on some staffing problems, and on the few occasions in which I came in contact with Stuart, he seemed very reserved—kind of cold, in fact. Later, of course, I found out how mistaken I'd been. Stuart is the best manager I've ever encountered, and I've worked with a lot. To start, he has a grasp of what's important. No matter what the topic is—how to get a skeptical customer to use our products, for instance—he'll see pieces of the problem that others have overlooked or haven't realized were important. And he can shift his focus from large scale to small without a hesitation.

Stuart is a very ethical person. He's a straight shooter when it counts, always speaking his mind, but the way he raises points is never raw—he's really disagreeing, but somehow it doesn't put you on edge. He has a very informal way about him, makes jokes at his own expense a lot, always listens to what others have to say in a way that makes you feel that he's genuinely interested, and I suppose he mostly is. Maybe that's why he's trusted at every level, above and below.

Is he political? Not in the back-stabbing or self-seeking way, but yes in that he keeps an eye on what others want and tries to connect with it. For instance, he knows that Frank, our COO, favors hardware. So every one of Stuart's proposals will show how what he wants to do will make better use of our hardware, or will help the hardware divisions, or will make our customer love hardware. I've personally found Stuart to be very helpful, but only if I ask. He doesn't volunteer help, and he doesn't push his ideas either. It's really a nice combination.

When I've suggested some new management method to him, he always listens (maybe a little skeptically), thinks about it for a while, and then—well, usually, anyway—he'll take some part of the idea and try it out. I've been advising managers and executives for twenty years, and I've never had anyone anywhere near that open to learning something new.

His hours? Stuart has never been a ten-hour-a-day man. Sure, he'll stay for a special job, but he likes to get home. His people, on the other hand, put in a lot of over-time and always feel overworked. I know Stuart worries about this, and I've been there when he's told them that he doesn't like it, doesn't do it himself, and doesn't expect them to do it. But I've wondered whether what happens is that he's so productive in his eight or nine hours that they're just trying to live up to his example. In this company we have about twenty managers at the director level, but he's the only one of that group—I'm excluding the senior managers—I would consider indis-pensable. I guess that includes myself.

It's never easy to tell another why a particular person seems special, and as this somewhat rambling narrative exemplifies, few interviewees were able to tie up their observations into neat, nicely inclusive bundles. So the categorized descriptions that follow result from our best efforts to abstract from a wealth of illustrative detail the essential qualities that distinguish indispensable people from their otherwise often highly competent peers. We considered an attribute to be a defining characteristic of indispensability if it was mentioned without cue by at least 50 percent of those interviewed. Since the open-ended interview format errs on the side of eliciting only what interviewees spontaneously recall, that same attribute might have been true for the others but was simply not thought of at the time of the interview. (In contrast, a direct-question format—"Was this person thoughtful?"—can induce the "recall" of qualities that may not be present at all.)

Although indispensable people differ from each other in almost every other way, nine personal characteristics make up the template against which one might match a potentially indispensable person:

1. They have an owner's perspective.

2. They are trustworthy and people of character.

3. They have a positive, can-do attitude.

4. They show a boundaried willingness to help others.

5. They relate well in certain specific ways.

6. They adapt well to change.

7. They clearly understand their organizational roles.

8. They are continuous learners.

9. They do not give their all to their organizations but opt for a balanced life. We inferred this quality from observations of IPs and from the fact that interviewees described them as keeping decent work hours ("He usually leaves the plant by 6:00 P.M."). For the last half of the interviews, we queried respondents directly on this point. None of the IPs worked unduly long hours unless special circumstances required it. On the other hand, none were small-business owners.

These qualities were mentioned so frequently, and with such similar details, that at times it seemed as if the same person were turning up in sixty different settings. For example, not only did almost every interviewee mention a willingness to be helpful, but everyone who mentioned this trait limited it with some version of "however, only when it was really needed." Indispensable people are evidently quite willing to assist their colleagues, but only when—in the IP's opinion, of course—that help is justified and somehow "deserved."

Early in my consulting career, my clients were chiefly the heads of small but growing businesses. They typically had complaints such as this one from the owner of a successful metal-plating company: "When I came in this morning, I found one of the tanks dangerously low in solvent, the cover askew on another tank, and there was George, who had gotten in ahead of me, unconcernedly preparing a new batch of fittings for replating. He walked by those two tanks on his way in, and I know that he knows the difference between a properly filled tank and one that's having a problem. How could he not stop to fix it? I just don't understand people who don't do what needs to be done."

My usual response was something on the order of "You expect your employees to feel the same way about this company that you do." Like other small-company CEOs who are concerned about everything and feel responsible for all of the business, the plating company owner was distressed that George, who was doing a first-rate job of everything his role called for him to do (prepare objects for plating), didn't also feel the same scope of responsibility. But, as George stoutly contended when I called him on his seeming obliviousness, it was too bad that someone had been careless about tank maintenance, but fixing it was not part of his job. (In fairness to employees like George, owners seldom realize how they promote this attitude, through many of their own actions—for example, giving summer jobs to members of their own families, but not extending that privilege to their employees. Although owners have a *right* to make that privilege exclusively theirs, the message is "This is my company; you only work here.")

It's easy to see why owners resent the "It's not my job" attitude. The organization they have worked so hard to establish and grow has really become part of themselves. With these sorts of experiences as background, as we heard repeated tales of how much indispensable people like Stuart Pickett seemed to *care*, we found ourselves thinking, "They sound just like owners."

Although IPs may sound like owners, they don't usually have a direct financial stake in the enterprise. So what is it about them that makes them look as if they do, making them attractive to owners and senior managers whose scope of responsibilities resembles that of an owner? Several specific traits emerged from our interviews: a focus on the mission of the whole enterprise, concern for the bottom line, and a feel for the hopes and anxieties of their bosses.

IPs Focus on the Mission of the Whole Enterprise

An owner's perspective is clearly more than simply having a strong work ethic, although that was often mentioned as a quality to be assumed in any good employee. All hardworking employees do their jobs as well as they can, try hard to meet the standards set for them by their organizations, and want to feel good about themselves and what they're doing. So the key distinguishing factor must be one of focus. For owners and those with an owner's perspective, the area of focus is the whole organization—small company, government agency, or corporate giant—and whatever is needed to keep it active and alive. Their more dispensable coworkers, perhaps as committed and energetic as they, focus almost exclusively on the mission of their own particular piece of the organization.

To put it simply, IPs do whatever needs doing, even if it's outside of their job descriptions or current assignments. Their bosses described that quality this way:

> I never heard him say anything like, "That's not my job." When a problem arose, he would do what he could and then make sure that others were brought in until it was fixed. I'm saying he would do that even when the problem wasn't part of his responsibility. It's what I do, of course, but this is my company. The amazing thing is that I usually found out about these things that Luiz did from others—sometimes from other managers who were complaining that he was stepping on their toes, when he was really doing them a favor.

Miguel would lean over backward to see what needed doing—not just his job—and then to see that it was done. Sometimes he got others pissed off at him because he wouldn't sit still until whatever needed fixing was fixed.

Officially she is a staff assistant—what we used to call a secretary—but she's willing to go outside her job description, if need be, to make sure that things get taken care of. For instance, last week she rousted an account salesman at home because a customer called late Friday with a problem. She could've just left a note on his desk for Monday, but she would never do that. Then she stayed at her desk until she was sure that Jack—the sales guy—wouldn't need information. What made her sore was that Jack didn't call her back to tell her that he'd taken care of the problem. But then he's not one of your indispensable people, although he is a pretty good salesman.

What I especially value is that he will go outside the box—whatever is needed to get the job done.

The following comment from one of these indispensable people seems to capture two aspects of this broader than usual focus: (1) that this perspective needs to be and can be learned, and (2) that achieving an owner's perspective is not always understood or appreciated by coworkers.

Sometimes you have to keep reminding yourself that what's best for you or your unit isn't always the right answer. Keep an eye on the common goal: what's best for the company, maybe even what's best for the country. I've noticed that this is hard to do—I don't expect all my peers will do it. But when I worked for a while on the CEO's quality task force, I found that I could do it. It's kind of a sign of the times that—I found this out later—some of the other people on the task force thought that I was weird because I suggested that other departments than mine get some of the work that was finally approved, and the budget goodies that went along with it. We could have done most of that work, and by rights it belonged in our department, but I thought others could do it either better or cheaper.

IPs Are Concerned with the Bottom Line

Everyone, in any organization we've ever encountered, was presumed to care about the fiscal health of the organization, but that concern actually is of prime interest only to those whose personal income is closely connected with how well the enterprise is doing. This is certainly true for managers, who are usually rewarded not for how well they manage—a phenomenon considered too difficult or too arduous to assess—but for the fiscal performance of their profit centers. Similarly, an outside salesperson's earnings depend upon the number of sales, and thus income, he or she generates for the company. But in both cases the focus of their attention is on their own bottom lines, rather than their contributions to overall profitability. What makes IPs stand out in their bosses' minds is that they show a concern for their organization's fiscal health, whether or not their own rewards are keyed to it. It's understandable that when owners or their executive stand-ins come across such an employee, they will see that person as very special.

I promoted Mickey to be chief financial officer solely because he was the only one of my direct reports who could look away from how well his division was doing to notice where this company was in its total balance sheet.

I can give Michelle a go-ahead on a project, knowing that she never forgets to balance the cost against the benefits. If she doesn't see a real payoff in a project she's working on—or, for that matter, in anyone's project, even mine—she'll propose shelving it. On the other hand, she always seems to be thinking about other sources of revenue, and Lord knows we need it, because our costs are constantly going up and we've reached a limit on what we can charge. What's really supportive for me is that I'm not the only one who's concerned about how we're going to make it.

In government agencies and other not-for-profit organizations, the equivalent is a determination to "stay within budget," a resolve not as commonly found as one might hope.

John's lab section has had its share of budget ups and downs, since funding levels seem to be set more by what's the "disease of the year" rather than any longer-term needs. Still, he's done the best job of staying one step ahead of the red ink. I wish I could say the same about my other lab chiefs.

IPs Have a Feel for Their Boss's Perspective

By and large, bosses are a rather worried lot. In part, it's simply tension over accomplishing results for which they are accountable. But even more worrisome are the ambiguities that float around how they are seen by their superiors. This uncertainty remains when one ascends the hierarchy; senior executive vice presidents puzzle over how they are seen by the CEO, even as their vice presidential underlings worry about what the senior vice president thinks of them. Decisions about promotions and resource allocation are difficult to make at best, and both good and bad unit performance is often due more to market swings than sterling or poor management. Consequently, perceptions are often as important as performance in determining who is seen as deserving of what. Managers may interpret chatting employees, an open magazine, or an engineer staring at the ceiling either as signs of inefficiency and lax management or as useful conferencing, work-related research, and that all-too-rare activity, creative thinking. Because most managers feel vulnerable to criticism, they appreciate employees who understand that appearances are realities unto themselves.

> Charlie is the one person around here I can talk to about the problem of coping with organizational pressures. I never worry that he's going to use anything I say to him in an underhanded way. If he thinks I'm wrong, he'll tell me. And most of all, he understands the importance of looking—as well as being—productive, profitable, and—in this division—team oriented.

Trustworthiness and Character

Trust is so much a matter of feeling and perception that it's often especially hard to say why some people seem more trustworthy than others. Here is one interview-ee's rather disjointed try at explaining why she was impressed with her IP's trustworthiness:

> What stands out about Mary is that she not only says straight out what she means, but if she tells you she'll get something done, she'll do it or tell you ahead of time that she can't—or won't—but that doesn't happen often. As I said, you can count on Mary. Of course, you'd like to be able to count on everybody, and most of the time you can, but there's something about Mary that gives an extra feeling of trust.

Indispensable people are an extraordinarily trusted lot, and it's hard to resist describing them as people of character. Three specific characteristics seem to provide the substance that underlies that trustworthi-ness: they are guided by their own high standards, they follow through on commitments, and they have a knack for communicating candidly without attack-ing or demeaning.

IPs Are Committed to Their Own High Standards

There is a seeming paradox about indispensable people. As problem solvers, they relish a diversity of perspec-tives, yet they were repeatedly described as committed to their own standards of competence, quality of ser-vice, and ethics, unwilling to abandon them even in the face of many pressures to compromise. To be able to do that in a world of cut corners and political intrigues requires strength of character, a key IP quality. These two quotes illustrate both the independence of mind and steadfastness that make IPs stand out:

> We do our work in a rather political environment; it's scrutinized by high-ranking military people, congressional staff who often represent completely opposite views, as well as government auditors and so on. Frankly, it's hard to keep a level head with all of that going on, given the fact that we're supposed to produce objective analysis and recommendations. The thing about Perry is that he seems to ride through all that without caring about what anyone else wants him to say or do. If he thinks he's right, he'll put it in the report, whether it will be popular with those who receive it or not. I don't mean that he's narrow-minded. He has lots of talks with almost everyone before he proceeds with writing up his studies, then he puts down what he believes and stands up for it until he thinks someone has shown him that he's wrong. I don't mean to imply that the rest of us simply pander to what others want us to come up with, but Perry seems the most unmoved by all the various winds that blow.

> She was willing to make unpopular decisions—to take a stand with prime focus on the mission of the organization. In my experience, doing that is very uncommon.

Based on comments by IPs' bosses and peers, as well as the behavior we have observed as consultants, IPs' decisions are influenced relatively little by matters irrelevant to the solution of problems, such as their bosses' preferred outcomes, cultural traditions or biases, academic theories on how things *should* work, reported experience, and even their own self-interests. IPs seem, in other words, more objective in their thinking. This greater objectivity may stem from the interaction of their inner-directedness with their paradoxical openness to differing perspectives.

In several conversations with IPs, it became clear that the ethical practices of the organizations in which they worked were a vital consideration to them. An indispensable nurse, after citing a number of her employer's poor management practices and lower than average pay scale, both of which she criticized, had this to say:

> I've stayed with this practice because I knew they were ethical. They never recommended treatment that wasn't needed, and they didn't pad their bills. They may have a lot of problems, but they're doing right.

Other IPs made similar comments:

> Do I feel loyalty to this company? Not to the owners or even to my bosses. I feel loyalty to what we do—to the service we provide—and to my clients.

> I believe in what this company does, and as a matter of fact, I think about it as "my company," and when we [the staff] are talking together, it's always "our company." But if I stop liking what we do here and I don't feel that way anymore, I'll leave, regardless of what it costs me.

IPs Follow Through on Commitments, but Only Those They Accept

IPs' extraordinary commitment to fulfilling the obligations they've accepted seemed to be particularly important to their coworkers. Interviewees often made the point that this quality was more than just a penchant for meeting deadlines, which was more or less expected of any good employee. IPs fulfill their obligations not because they are required to, but because they feel personally bound by them. For that reason, they are as selective as they can be about which obligations they'll accept, always keeping an eye on the reality that even when all of one's tasks are important, some are still more important than others.

To meet your commitments while maintaining high standards of accomplishment in a world of constant pressures for growth, ever-increasing profitability, and tight resources requires a variety of streetwise skills for wending one's way through the practicalities of everyday organizational life. For example, a world in which needs often outpace resources demands a commitment to keeping priorities straight, slacking off on the less important to be able to accumulate the time and money to do a first-rate job on the more important. It was not by chance that, without prompting, over one-third of our interviewees cited adeptness at prioritizing as one of the ancillary characteristics of their IPs.

> I could depend on her to come through with whatever it was she said she would do.

> If she says it can't be done in the time allotted, I believe her, because if it could be done, I know she would do it.

> If he thinks a deadline is unrealistic, he'll tell me so and almost always will negotiate a new completion time. What I can count on is that he will make that deadline

or he'll tell me why he can't in plenty of time to do something about it. What I don't need to worry about is that the deadline will slip by without my hearing from him.

When he told you that something needed fixing, or that it couldn't be fixed, you believed him. Sure, I checked every once in a while, because it was my job. Actually, it got to be a game in which I tried to catch him up—but I never did.

IPs Communicate Candidly Without Attacking

Indispensable people seem to be an unusually candid lot, openly voicing their concerns or disagreements without subterfuge, yet they do it in a way that doesn't attack or demean those with whom they disagree. There is much evidence that openness in communication tends to foster trust in others, but only if those others don't feel disparaged by what was said or how it was delivered. Since IPs stand up for whatever they think is right, or for the best solution to a problem, it is especially important for them to learn how to be firm without putting others off. That they have done so is surely an important reason why bosses and coworkers value them so highly.

He's the one I go to when I have a problem. He won't snow me; he's a straight shooter.

She could respect and honor people with whom she disagreed. She would listen and then show them why she disagreed, but never put them down.

Sherry never says, "You're stupid." Instead she'll say, "I'm uncomfortable with that," and then tell you why, or she'll say, "You may be right, but could you walk a little way down this path to see if it works for you, too?" It's hard to be mad at her even when you know that you're losing the argument.

You always know where Ken is coming from—no bullshit. But he has this nice way of telling you so you somehow don't resent it. I've tried to learn how to do that by watching him. It's like you just say what's on your mind without arguing that the other person is wrong. I'm a better manager for it.

In an oversimplified way, one might say that IPs have learned the knack of being assertive without seeming aggressive.

Positive but Realistic Can-Do Attitude

IPs confidently tackle problems or projects regardless of difficulty or complexity. A common shorthand for this quality was "a can-do attitude," expressed in a variety of ways. Psychologists call this attitude self-efficacy, meaning the extent to which you believe that you can successfully manage the problems that come your way—as distinguished from self-esteem, or the extent to which you believe you have value as a person. You can have high self-esteem but low self-efficacy, and vice versa. Thus, you might have a high opinion of yourself in a general way but doubt your ability to solve complex mathematical problems, or you can view yourself as a whiz at math yet give yourself little value as a person. An apt generalization would be that IPs may vary in the degree to which they generally esteem themselves—some quite modest, even retiring, while most probably think pretty well of themselves—but they all have acquired confidence in their ability to accomplish a lot. This is a sort of grounded optimism—not that the world is all sunshine, but that persistence and the application of their mental and interpersonal skills will usually prevail.

Psychological studies of optimism and pessimism as personality traits show that pessimists are generally more in touch with all of the ramifications of reality than their more positively thinking fellows. However, most successful people tend to assume a rosy future, and doing so usually pays off for them. An optimistic perceptual bias boosts people's willingness to strike out into unknown territory, pursue ventures in the face of obstacles, and—perhaps even more important—persevere until they push through. But there is also evidence that an overly optimistic view, unsupported by cautious good sense, can lead people to waste resources in pursuit of unattainable goals. Indispensable people, in contrast, combine confidence in their ability to make headway against even formidable problems with an inclination to pay attention to a broad range of views, even those of dedicated negativists, a potent perceptual combination.

> He's very upbeat. He seems to think there must be an answer to any problem and he can find it.

She's trained herself to be an upbeat, can-do kind of person.

What's unusual about him as a controller is that he has a can-do attitude while at the same time he's very careful about not bending the rules. Many controllers get caught up in doing things right, rather than doing the right thing. He does both.

If Mattie says it can't be done, I can believe her, because she looks every which way for some way to accomplish what she needs to.

The thing about Millie is that she is very proactive. She doesn't wait to be told how to handle a problem; she just goes ahead and does something, and it usually turns out to be right. I just never have to tell her what to do.

Anne just has what I call a very positivistic—that's the opposite of negativistic—way of seeing things. She's not one to say, "You can't get there from here."

Ability to Relate Well in Certain Specific Ways

It was not surprising to us that interviewees characterized indispensable people as relating well in certain specific ways. What we didn't expect was how different they were in most other ways. For example, many were fleshed out as extroverts; others came across as quietly introverted. Some were friendly and effervescent; others businesslike almost to the point of brusqueness. Some were team oriented; others preferred to work alone. Indispensable people do relate well with those with whom they work, but they are similar only in certain specific ways: they are respectful listeners, they are not defensive or blaming, and they have little status consciousness.

IPs Listen Respectfully

Indispensable people listen attentively. They treat others, including those who report directly to them, as equals, thus making the people they deal with feel respected and taken seriously, regardless of differences in background, age, or social position.

> He listens to what you have to say, even when he's just argued against it.

> She would talk to you in a way that was personal. You felt really listened to.

> She could respect and honor people with whom she disagreed—even disliked.

> Others felt understood by her. She was the boss all right, but she had the same demeanor with everyone.

> He couldn't speak English very well, but he worked hard at understanding what they were trying to do, and somehow he seemed to be able to communicate with everyone he had to work with.

She could relate well to all of the leaders in the community, professionals, corporate people, labor reps, workers, gays, gang members, everyone. She always listened to them straight through and made sure she understood what they wanted. It was time-consuming, but it worked.

She's already a project leader because she's able to bring people together—to keep people talking, to mediate disagreements. It's a real gift, keeping cool but not letting go of the fact that disagreements can be, and will be, resolved.

In her quiet way she's always been really appreciative of others' efforts, and she shows it, but she doesn't flatter or throw out phony togetherness talk.

IPs Are Not Defensive or Blaming

Many interviewees made the point that the indispensable person they were describing did not try to foist responsibility on others, even when accusations were being tossed around. They obviously admired this nondefensive, nonblaming attitude.

You wouldn't believe how unusual it is to find someone who doesn't react defensively when a problem is brought up by me, by one of the other staff, or by a customer.

Sure, if I don't do something important because I wasn't on track or I wasn't focused enough, Samantha's right out there telling me just how I've goofed, and she gets just as furious at herself when she's let something slip by. But then she lets it go. All she wants to know is,

What do we do now to fix it? I think I like that more than anything else.

What I really appreciated most when Jake worked for me—and I still do, even though we're now equal-level managers—is that he is not one to try to explain away something that's gone wrong. He just won't defend himself. He simply listens to all the scrambling when there's been a problem, then starts talking about how to fix it. I don't mean that he tries to get out from under his responsibility; he just seems to assume that whose fault it was is irrelevant.

IPs Are Skilled at Mediating Disagreements

IPs in management and professional positions are skilled at mediating disagreements. Many interviewees specifically mentioned this ability.

Since our whole business is developing analyses and action plans concerning complex problems about which everyone has an opinion, what I most value about Trev is that he can sit down with a bunch of deep but narrow experts and get them to agree on something they can all support.

Often interviewees only alluded to this skill:

Geri will sit down with her people to divide up something like department travel funds. There's often a lot of squabbling about that, but she works with them and works with them until they have a plan they'll all buy.

A skill at mediating disagreements is characteristic of indispensable people, although others may not notice it until IPs have arrived at managerial or senior staff positions. It is, perhaps, a secondary trait, a by-product of a broad-gauged intellect, receptive to divergent viewpoints, and an ability to disagree without deprecating, seasoned by belief that all problems are amenable to productive resolution.

IPs Are Not Status-Conscious

Like Henry Higgins, who in Shaw's play *Pygmalion* (later reincarnated as *My Fair Lady*) claimed to have a democratic nature because he treated duchesses and flower girls with equal rudeness, indispensable people seem to have learned that the best way to handle hierarchical relationships is to relate to others as if differences in authority did not imply social distance. Regardless of the position of those with whom they are interacting, they are neither deferent nor haughty, neither arrogant nor unduly apprehensive. They are simply people doing business together. Not only does this behavior send an egalitarian message, but persons of power tend to interpret the apparently comfortable self-confidence as a sign of strength.

> She has this matter-of-fact attitude toward everyone. I mean she talks just the same to the CEO and to the support people.

> He was team leader of a small assembly crew, and I was the general manager. He didn't speak English very well— had a heavy accent—but when I was down on the floor

looking at some kind of problem that his bunch was involved with, he would explain to me very clearly what had happened, what he thought was wrong, and what he planned to do about it. If I put my two cents in and he disagreed, he would just tell me, "No, Arnold, we can't do it that way," with no beating around the bush. But he was never in your face about it. We were just two guys talking together. I made him a foreman even though his background was less than what we ordinarily looked for.

I always envied her because she was the same with everyone, no matter who they were. We used to get visits—you know, visiting dignitaries, very important people, sometimes real celebrities—and she would speak with them as if they were anyone. I would get all tongue-tied and stupid, and they would patronize me as if I were a nobody instead of the principal investigator of important research.

Was it her manner with those "distinguished visitors" that got her moved to the prestigious position she's in? Not completely, of course. She was an exceptional person and a competent scientist, but then we've got lots of those here.

Willingness to Help Others, Within Boundaries

Indispensable people are often chosen as mentors, those to whom one goes for information, advice, or help, and they are generous with that help, but only when it is asked for and needed. Ips are not busybodies, intruding into coworkers' work space, nor do they assume that a colleague or subordinate who is struggling with a task ought to be rescued. However, when asked, they are usually more than willing to provide assistance and support *if* they believe that their help will further some clear organizational need and that those asking for help have gone as far as they were able to accomplish the task on their own. IPs, it would seem, apply their own high standards of effort and performance to others.

> He helps anyone who really needs his help, but he's not just a patsy. I mean I've heard him say, "You don't really need me," to Garth, who was the weakest of all the foremen—but he does it so nicely.

> She could and did set boundaries. Binnie would be helpful but not do others' work for them.

> Maria had limits on how much help she would give. She would be helpful but not do others' work for them.

> He could be stingy with his time when he was busy himself, but in such a way that it was not seen as a negative, but as his merely being very focused.

> We go to Gary for answers all the time, but he doesn't waste time—that is, he doesn't chat us up. Gary's nice enough, but he's very no-nonsense.

> She's willing to teach anyone who asks. She doesn't hoard her knowledge, but she'll let you struggle with it without taking it out of your hands. And as soon as you've begun to get it, she moves on to other things.

Adaptability to Change

The ability to weather changing conditions without agonizing over them is a prized attribute of indispensable people. It is likely a product of more fundamental traits. A broad perspective certainly helps to place the disruptions that are always part of any significant change in context. Mental flexibility and a willingness to do the next indicated thing can mitigate the painful sense of loss when comfortably old ways are discarded. Because IPs invest their loyalty and commitment in the goals and accomplishments of their organization, rather than in the organization itself, they are likely to feel less demoralized by a merger, acquisition, or restructuring.

As I write this, I am consulting with an organization that is reeling from a complete overhaul of its goals, structure, and long-established culture. Those few—as they always are—indispensable people in the groups with which I am working clearly are responding to the often chaotic conditions as an opportunity for genuine improvement in product and service, and for personal development. It is for them a time of high adventure, not of loss.

All three of the people I've mentioned were not afraid of change. I don't mean they like change for its own sake, but when it occurred, they would deal with it without a lot of fuss.

He is able to handle different jobs that come up. I mean he will graciously move to a new task when need be. He does this for me and for others on the floor.

She's not afraid of change. She doesn't invite it or provoke it, but when it arrives, she works with it without a lot of fuss.

Our company has gone through a lot over the past five years. We grew fast, were acquired by a conglomerate, and then were sold to the outfit we're with now, and every time, there were huge changes—at least they seemed that way. A lot of good people were let go. Rich worked for me for two years, moved laterally when we were bought, and is now my boss. The thing that I relish most about him is that all this garbage never seemed to faze him. He has saved me, and I think many others, from real depression.

How? It's not so much what he says—actually he's a kind of quiet guy—as a feeling that for him changes come with the territory and that anyway it's all part of a big joke. That sounds as if he doesn't care, but of course he always does a top job.

Understand Their Organizational Roles

If it's true, as French novelist and statesman André Malraux once suggested, that intelligence is "knowing how to play your role in the play," then one would have to accord IPs still another sort of intelligence. They appear to have a deeper than usual grasp of their place in the organizational scheme of things. Although many of the pertinent interview comments were either tangential or specific to only one aspect of organizational role, together they created an impression of IPs as acutely aware of the complexities of organizational life, making conscious choices about how they want to fit into that complexity.

The result seems to be a relationship that is both comfortable and distanced. IPs don't take themselves or their organizations too seriously, but they care much for the quality of products and services that the organization provides. That may be why, as managers, IPs seldom are the target of the three most common complaints directed at that group: entanglement in those struggles over tasks and resources known as "turf wars," failure to delegate well, and failure to inform others in the organization about matters that might affect them.

IPs Are Not Turf-Conscious

IPs focus on the success of the whole enterprise rather than just their piece of it. That is probably the major reason why they seem so little concerned with *who* in their organization does what needs to be done, and so much concerned with how well it is done. Ironically, because IPs show so little interest in aggrandizing their own units, others are often inclined to ask them to take on increased responsibilities.

> John is definitely not territorial. At staff meetings, when the group is parceling out new jobs that might fit into his bailiwick or into Mary's, he will say, "I think Mary has better people for this. Why not give it to her?"

> Samantha didn't ever have to win when accounts were being assigned. She never drew a line in the sand and said, "This belongs to me." Not just in public, either. As far as she was concerned, getting the work out was more important than who did it. Of course, I don't think we ever lost any good jobs anyway.

IPs Delegate Well

Every manager avows the merits of delegating—tasks along with the authority needed to complete them. Hardly any have difficulty with the assignment part, but many inwardly agonize about truly giving up control over how the tasks should be done. Among the many reasons cited to explain—or excuse—incomplete delegation are too strong a need for personal power, lack of confidence in subordinates, and perfectionist fears that mistakes will be made. However, none of these problems seem to plague indispensable managers.

> Al was not driven by a need to do things himself that others could do. He saved himself for what he could do best.

> What was special about her was that she gave me a lot of leeway to get my job done, but she was always there when I needed to talk something over. What stands out for me is that in our one-on-ones, even when it was obvious that I was unsure of what to do next, she never tried to take over the decision.

> Every one of the five people I've told you about is a real delegator. They keep an eye on how things turn out and do what they need to do to prevent the same mistakes from happening, but they let their people have all the authority they need to get the job done. I consider that part of their can-do approach.

IPs Keep Others Informed

Keeping others informed without overinforming them—isn't information overload the organizational malady of this decade?—takes thought, planning, and a respect for the value of their concerns and potential contributions. It is probably always incompletely done, but IPs seem to do a better job than most, likely a result of their concern for the effectiveness of the entire enterprise and a feel for how their own work interconnects with that of even distant others.

> He always keeps people in the loop.

> She made a point of asking who would be affected by any of the letters we sent out to providers, county health people, and other state agencies. Everyone would get some kind of notice about what we were doing. "Surprised people are resentful people" was sort of her motto—we heard it often enough—but she was right. She kept her own staff informed, too.

An IP described her own behavior this way:

> I travel back and forth among our offices and keep huge jobs going. People know me and trust me. I communicate.

Continuous Learning

Both IPs and their bosses saw a penchant for learning as an almost taken for granted aspect of indispensability. Two bosses expressed that attribute this way:

> She did not resist new technology. She learned what was needed, or directed someone on her staff to learn it and then teach her what she needed to know.

> If he doesn't know an answer, he'll go look it up. He reads
> all the time, corners visiting experts, and not just about
> his own specialty. And, remember, I'm talking about a
> mechanic, not an engineer or a college professor.

The following comments represent IPs' self-perceptions:

> I've done cross-training, I keep taking CE courses, and I
> always will, I guess. And you never know when what you
> learn will come in handy. When I was secretary of the
> local chapter of my professional organization, I learned
> word processing. Now I've become the computer
> "expert" in our little company.

> The cross-training I've had has given me a good feeling
> for every other job that affects mine. I appreciate what
> they do and can be really helpful when an emergency
> arises. It's also given me a better sense of how all the
> pieces fit together—or at least ought to.

Leading Balanced Lives

It is certainly characteristic of IPs to work hard when
they are working. We heard "She has a work ethic" in
almost every interview. Still, they generally try to keep
reasonable work hours. When they do not, it is often
because that tantalizing goal of doing a job excellently
has pulled them along past their normal working hours.
Perhaps this makes IPs tend toward what some psychologists have called achievement-oriented (rather than
compulsive-dependent or perfectionist) workaholism—
in balance, a failing probably more positive than negative. The point is that IPs seem to be motivated to put

in extra hours by their own assessment of what is needed for high-quality completion of the task, rather than by a need for approval or fear of any consequences. For more on this subject see Scott, K., et al., in the References section at the back of the book.

After several of our first interviewees made the point that their indispensable people were seldom late-hour drones, we began to ask whether IPs typically worked long hours. The almost invariable response—"not unless there is a special reason to do so"—is well reflected in the following comments:

> He's family-oriented—only works eight to nine hours a day. Of course, if there's a major project deadline (a real one, not just an administrative one), he does what's needed—weekends or sometimes all night.

> At this company it seems that almost every manager turns in ten- or twelve-hour days; there are tons of paperwork, and it's the expected thing. So when I say that Arnold doesn't do that, it says something about him—he goes his own way. It also says that the rest of us must be spending too much time at work.

> The thing I most respect about her is that she seems to keep a balance in her life. She stays late and on weekends when it's really needed but otherwise gets out at five, maybe six, every night.

Necessary but Not Sufficient Attributes

Two additional attributes did not in themselves differentiate IPs from their colleagues but seemed necessary for someone to even be considered indispensable. The first attribute was a reasonable level of technical competence, and the second was dependability.

Reasonable Competence

When we asked directly about the importance of technical competence in the various jobs for which the IPs had been hired, the typical response was that they were never the most skillful or technically knowledgeable. Frequently our informants added that what marked an indispensable person was broad knowledge, rather than deep knowledge in a specific area.

> Sure, Dave's competence got him in the door, but there are lots of competent people who are not indispensable. When the business area that uses their competence slows down, they have to be let go. It's the other qualities that Dave has that make him so valuable.

> He knew what he was doing but certainly wasn't the most technically competent. I've been sitting here thinking about the most knowledgeable person and why I don't see her as indispensable. In part, it's because she doesn't seem to use what she knows as well. You know, around here it's all about solving problems and figuring out what's wrong. Maybe knowing too much gets in the way of that.

> It's definitely not just competence, unless maybe some kind of genius or supercreative person. You have to have a reasonable amount of know-how, but I have a lot of technically competent people who are contributors, but they can be replaced.

> The indispensable people I've mentioned have a broad competency rather than a deep competency. We need

people like that too, but they are not the ones we can't do without.

Ordinary Dependability

Interviewees seldom mentioned dependability as an indispensable quality. When we asked them about it directly, they would point out that getting assignments in on time and showing up were the responsibility of any employee, indispensable or not. Interviewees recognized that this expectation was not always met, but still, they did not think of dependability as a distinguishing mark of an indispensable person. Of course, lack of dependability would rule out an employee as indispensable.

> Well, we do need people who close on their assignments, and there are sure some who don't. It's very desirable in an employee, but does it make them indispensable? No.

> If you'd asked me what makes a good employee, I would have put dependability near the top, but most of my people are pretty good about that most of the time, Frank included. But what makes him stand out is something different—actually a lot of things different.

Irrelevant or Negative Qualities

Several attributes that often turn up in discussions about employees seem to be irrelevant to indispensability, or even to have a negative tinge. The irrelevant and negative attributes we identified are personal popularity, creativity, and difficult or disruptive behavior patterns.

Personal Charm or Popularity with Staff

While nice people are welcome in any workplace, "niceness" in itself seems irrelevant to indispensability.

> Sheila is charming and quite attractive—in our line of work [entertainment industry] we get a lot like that—but that's not what makes her indispensable.

> Charlie is the life of the party, remembers birthdays, always good for a laugh. I like to have him around, and everybody else does, too. I'd hate to let him go, but I would—he's not indispensable.

Creativity Alone

We were surprised that creativity—a knack for generating new or imaginative ideas—was not once mentioned as an indispensable quality. It is certainly not true that organizations, including those in our sample, can do without the unique perspectives of creative people to spark new ideas and innovation. Rather, we suspect, employees who are seen as bedrock to the organization show a steadiness and "all-aroundness" that people do not associate with extraordinary creativity.

While imagination is often held out to be a great virtue, creative people who lack a systems view and the ability to integrate a variety of perspectives are not likely to be seen as indispensable. That may be the reason why some organizations, having at length engineered an idea into a practical, sellable, and highly profitable product, have shabbily treated the truly creative individual whose idea it was.

Disruptive or Difficult Behavior

Difficult or disruptive behavior patterns such as abrasiveness, an explosive temper, or chronic indecision will disqualify an otherwise superior employee from being indispensable. Such behavioral flaws are often tolerated in technically able workers. However, frequent complaints from subordinates or coworkers will make these difficult employees tempting targets when mergers or other organizational changes set up easy outplacements.

A Few Comments About Wanna-Bes

Although indispensable people choose not to work overly long hours, except to meet important deadlines, some interviewees ascribed seventy-hour weeks to employees who hoped to be seen as indispensable—the wanna-bes, as one interviewee referred to them. There were other differences between the wanna-bes and the true articles, of course. These are the missteps understandable as the struggles of ambitious—or worried—people who based their efforts on an erroneous assumption of what truly indispensable people are like.

The first of the following two examples describes a CEO's impressions of a general manager:

> Jed is very dependable; he works a huge number of hours, and he's proud of that. He thinks that's the way to impress me, but he's way off target. Right now we're expanding, and I need everyone I can get with management experience, but if things got tight, I'd merge his division in with Tom's and let him go. Any manager who works ten, twelve hours a day obviously doesn't know how to delegate. You know, when I told Jed that I've never worked more than eight hours a day, he was shocked. What I didn't tell him was that although I show up for eight hours, all I've really given any organization was a solid six hours a day, and it's always been enough.

> Nancy would like to make herself indispensable, but a lot of things she does have the opposite effect. For instance, she's in charge of contracting, so she hoards every little piece of the work connected with contracting. She's embellished what should be a simple process so much that it takes forever to get a contract out. The result is she stays late every day just to keep up, and tells everyone—with words and looks—about how hard she's working.

What Makes IPs Unique

Taken by itself, none of the attributes of IPs is rare. Any one, two, or three might be found in any competent employee, yet not convey an aura of indispensability. The thing that marks a person as a special, one out of ten (or one hundred), indispensable person must be the combination of all or most of these qualities. Certainly, IPs are not always seen as "nice" people. They are at times impatient, severe, businesslike to the point of brusqueness, and honest when others wish they weren't.

Perhaps a partial answer to the question of what makes IPs seem unique is to be found in an essay, "The Hedgehog and the Fox," by the late philosopher Sir Isaiah Berlin. Striking out from an ancient proverb (attributed to Archilochues, a sage of the seventh century B.C.)—"The fox knows many things, but the hedgehog knows only one great thing"—Berlin suggests that greatness can spring from a single splendid talent or from the right cluster of important but lesser abilities. Indispensable people certainly seem to be of the fox persuasion—more than a little accomplished at many things but seldom the best at any one.

A Guild Perspective

In addition, we believe there is something more to being indispensable: IPs have a particular perspective on their personal relationship to work and to the organization with which they've cast their lot. We might think of this perspective as a "guild perspective." IPs seem to have defined themselves as if they were working out of the craft guilds that were the powerful work engines five hundred years ago.

Toward the end of the Middle Ages, taking a lesson from the powerful merchant guilds that preceded them, artisans of every sort formed themselves into craft guilds. They set and maintained high standards and equally high levels of remuneration. Guild members worked independently, moving from assignment to assignment but always bound by the rules of conduct of their respective guilds. Their identification was with the art that only they, or other members of their guild, could practice—not with the person or organization that had retained them.

Then, as now, guild membership was the perfect stance for one working in a world of tremendous economic transition. Investing loyalty in organizations that are on the move, downsizing, relocating, expanding, being shoved along by turbulent technology changes is likely to lead more to hurt and disappointment than to the emotional stability anyone needs to do his or her best work. A much sounder basis for a sense of identity and personal worth is a commitment to one's self and to doing what one does—one's craft—as well as possible.

In our conversations with IPs, the underlying theme was always "I do the job right because that's what I do." From that perspective, an "owner's mentality" is a misnomer. The IP's allegiance is not to the owner or to the organization at all, but to the work to be done, the problems to be solved, the goals to be reached. In fact, as IPs have emphasized—and we have seen them do it—when conditions are such that they are not free to practice their craft well, they leave. (Of course, it's easier for them because they are so employable.)

This perspective frees them from the usual bureaucratic entanglements—turf battles, status and position, nonproductive competition. IPs do compete for higher-level positions, but usually it is to avoid being bound by the negative aspects of their organization's culture. As one reluctant IP said to us about acceding to his boss's request that he throw his hat in the promotional ring, "I don't want to be a paper-pushing vice president, but I know who else is in the running. If I don't take the job, this division will become like the others—ordinary." He was right.

Does the Nature of the Job Make a Difference?

Does the nature of your job determine the qualities that would make you indispensable? Common sense would say that the answer must be yes, but taken as a whole, the results of our interviews suggest a more ambiguous conclusion. Given the frequency with which they were mentioned, all of the qualities we have covered in Chapters 2 and 3 seem to contribute to indispensability. But the degree to which each is valued clearly depends upon the nature of the job to be done. An owner's perspective and an inclination toward mentoring may be vital to a department store floor manager's aura of indispensability, but it is somewhat less important to a production manager, for whom a systems view might be a key quality. Yet, since the cluster of all or most of the qualities is what marks out the indispensable few, a production manager without a reasonable dose of an owner's perspective and a mentoring mentality would be excluded from the ranks of the indispensable.

What Shapes Indispensability?

Indispensable people don't think of themselves as such, but when we asked them to ruminate about significant events in their own development, a few commonalities emerged. Most recalled certain pivotal experiences that made a difference in the way they felt about themselves as working human beings.

Mentors

Many IPs developed important qualities in response to the influence of parents, teachers, and other mentors. Here are some examples, each from a different IP:

> My first five years on the job, I moved like a whirlwind. I took on every assignment I could, thought of myself as a hotshot, didn't ask for help, and didn't give much either. I came down to earth when my boss—he was quite a bit older—gave some of my responsibilities to another engineer and said some things I've never forgotten. At first, of course, I was insulted, then I realized that he meant it when he said they just didn't want to lose me. It changed my whole philosophy, and I learned some wisdom about what makes you really valuable: don't hoard your knowledge, take whatever help you need to get the job done. It made me a better person and coworker.

> Two things happened to me when I was a kid that made a huge difference. I had a teacher in elementary school who stopped me after I'd delivered what I thought was a great book report. I still remember exactly what she said: "No, no—you've told us what the story is, but what is it all

about?" Later, when I was in high school, my mother, who was fascinated by foreign languages, sat down with me once after I'd complained about doing assignments, talked to me about understanding a language, where it came from, what the people who spoke that language were like. I began to see that studying a language was not just daily drudge work or even gaining facility in it. I think what I began to see was that the extra effort I started putting in made learning the language more enjoyable. I've forgotten most of what happened back then, but as you can see, after forty-five years those memories are still with me.

My father was very good to me, but he was never satisfied with anything that I did—it was never good enough. I hated that, and thinking about it is still painful to me, but I must say that it made me someone who invariably does more than what's required.

Two things come to mind that had an influence on me. Once, when I was in school, I was completely overwhelmed by having to prepare a science project for the annual science fair. Since I was obviously coming apart, my science teacher—really a very wise person—sat me down and told me a story, the punch line of which was "This too will pass." That line has kept me calm during crises more times than I can say.

The second event happened after I'd been working in a research lab. I was just a technician then, and one of my duties was to keep records. Well, to put it mildly, I was lax about that, and when my boss discovered it, he sat me down and read me the riot act. Getting scolded was no fun; I mean, I had been in the service, I wasn't just a kid, but what was really bad was the disappointment he had in me. Somehow it made it clear to me that there was more to a job than just following orders and getting by.

Breadth of Experience

A second commonality, mentioned both by IPs and by their bosses, was a series of diverse job experiences that exposed them to differing perspectives. For instance, when we asked an IP to explain his ability to draw consensus from a discordant group of experts, he credited his work experience:

> As a marine officer, you have one foot on sea and one foot on shore. That is, you learn to see things through the eyes of a soldier but also from the eyes of the navy guys, who have different goals and different problems to solve.

Another IP gained broad experience in the world of journalism:

> My first job was as a reporter on a small newspaper, and I often had the assignment of being the sole person around to finalize the Sunday edition. You learn as much about your own job as you can, but then you learn about every other job you bump up against. You see how different the problems are in all the other departments.

It seems safe to say that indispensability does not evolve through narrow experience, no matter how expert in that particular specialty one becomes.

Genetics and IP Qualities

Do some of the characteristics that distinguish IPs have a genetic substrate? Possibly. Recent studies of identical twins suggest that at least 50 percent of one's motivational inclinations, and even some patterns of thought, are to some extent inherited. For example, aggressiveness as a general trait seems to have a genetic basis, as does the tendency to be nurturing and community-oriented. It's also true that some difficult behaviors like bullying and indecisiveness are often the result of an overuse of inherent feistiness or solicitousness.

Still, the way you express your human nature is within your control, even when your biology is pushing you to deal roughly with the opposition or to muddy the truth to avoid distressing someone who deserves to be distressed. For example, when engaged in a struggle, you can choose to define your opposition as a recalcitrant situation, rather than a recalcitrant person. If so, you'll leap quickly to get information from as many sources as you can, rather than going for your opponent's jugular. IPs, while certainly assertive enough when something of importance is at stake, focus their aggressiveness on solving problems or mediating disagreements. It is impossible to know whether they were fortunate enough to have inherited all their motivations in balance, or whether they simply learned to modulate their more extreme innate tendencies. However, because IPs differ widely in the degree to which they show some traits thought to be partially inherited, such as whether they are extroverted or introverted, indispensability seems to be mostly acquired rather than inborn.

Our own conclusion is certainly that the skills and attitudes that add such high value to indispensable people can be learned, relearned, embellished, or modified by anyone who is willing to push aside old interfering habits of mind in order to open the way to a new and exciting work life. But that is not always easy to do.

I had met Mike Geber at one of his boss's off-site meetings, so I wasn't completely surprised by his E-mail note asking me to stop by. "Things are getting crazy around here, Dr. Bramson," he blurted, even before I found a seat in his small office, "and I'd like to make sure I survive the upcoming deconstruction."

Before this meeting, I'd heard some things about Mike, mostly from Al, his boss. Mike was a talented, aggressive engineering manager with a reputation on high as "a self-seeking empire builder," and the general opinion was that he had hit his promotional ceiling. The accusations were true enough, Al had remarked. Mike had pushed his own unit's interest at every opportunity and had made it known that he was ready to move into a director's slot. The "deconstruction" he referred to was indeed a plan for a major organizational restructuring on the horizon.

"I like working for this company," Mike said. "I have a new house, a new baby, and a wife who doesn't want to move. But the last time I prodded Al about a promotion, he finally told me about the bad rep I acquired in Building 1. Until a few days ago, I was so pissed I was thinking of resigning. But I don't really want to, and Shirley certainly doesn't want me to. What I want to do is to show them that I'm too good to let go when they start dropping off surplus mangers. Al said I could have a few hours with you to help me figure out what to do."

Since I'd just finished my first batch of indispensable-people interviews, I had a lot to tell Mike. He glumly digested my summary of what those highly valued people were like, obviously discouraged. "That's going to take some work, isn't it? Is it really worth it?" So for the next hour we talked about pros, cons, and possibilities. I encouraged him to seriously question whether the size of the effort was worth it.

Changing yourself significantly is often a testy proposition, doubly so when you do it without much outside pressure. After all, laid off or not, Mike would still be highly employable. He'd rather not switch jobs, but if he had to, he could without a horrendous cost. At length, he decided to go for it, and a year later he was glad he did. How he managed to accomplish his makeover, and how you can decide whether or not to embark on that course yourself, are the subject of the next chapter.

Becoming an Indispensable Person

FROM THE DESCRIPTION in Section I, would you conclude that you are already indispensable to your employer? If so, congratulations! However, most of us have room to develop. The chapters in this section show you how to plan to become a more indispensable person in your company. Chapter 4 sets the stage by outlining the benefits and costs of acquiring an aura of indispensability. It lays out the challenge by providing a questionnaire you can use to decide what you still need to learn. Chapter 5 details an approach you can use to plan your own development program.

4

Creating an Indispensable-Person Role for Yourself

So you're seriously contemplating remaking yourself into an indispensable person? To make a genuine commitment—and no other kind will do—an essential step is to consider reasons for *not* doing so. Surely there will be some drawbacks, if only the discomfort of stretching your mind to fit new perspectives. As certainly, a host of good things will come your way as you begin to accrue the characteristics of an indispensable person. Let's start by reviewing the benefits.

Reasons for Becoming an IP

Most of the advantages of being an IP involve the good feelings that go with self-respect and job security.

Protection from Layoff

If you are the kind of employee we call indispensable, then your organization won't even consider laying you off until its "dispensable" employees are gone. No matter how drastically your organization prunes itself, 80 percent of your coworkers will have to go before your name will come up. Recall that the most liberal estimate qualified no more than 10 percent as indispensable. To be conservative, we are adding an extra 10 percent to allow for personal favoritism, family connections, and other unfair factors.

First Hired

Indispensable people are not only the last fired, but also the first hired. Even before you need to pursue another job, you'll have received job offers from clients, customers, and vendors who've observed you in action or have seen the high regard in which your colleagues and present employers hold you. For example, this letter of recommendation was written by one IP's boss to a prospective employer:

> I write this letter burdened by great ambivalence. Robert wants advancement to a level that we simply cannot offer, although we've offered him just about everything else. He is one of the best employees I've ever had. He always goes for quality, he gets the important things done, he is very insightful when it comes to solving problems, he is both a team player and an independent worker, he is realistic yet very positive, he's looked up to by most of us around here for advice and counsel. All in all I hope you decide not to take him, because then we might be able to woo him back.

Respect from Coworkers

As an IP, you will enjoy a particular kind of respect from most of your coworkers. They will see you as a support to them rather than as a competitor. They'll come to you for counsel and mentoring, and they will be genuinely pleased when you receive kudos, in part because you're so willing to share the glory.

An Inner Sense of Worth

If you become an IP, you will feel an inner sense of worth, independent of affirmation from others. That feeling will keep you afloat even in those moments of doubt that we all experience.

Extrinsic Rewards

Will you also gain extrinsic rewards—raises, bonuses, stock options? Probably yes, but maybe no. Most indispensable people are seen as great assets to team performance, and if your organization bases bonuses on team as well as individual performance, you may add significantly to your income. However, extrinsic rewards often depend on hierarchical level, and since IPs seldom accept unpleasant or uninteresting assignments just for more pay, greater remuneration may depend upon your personal interest in becoming a practicing manager and whether your style of leadership is currently fashionable in your organization.

Of course, rewards will also depend on whether or not your immediate bosses are secure enough to be unworried that you might supplant them. If faced with that distasteful situation, however, every IP we've known has taken advantage of the "first hired" aura and simply moved to an even better job.

Reasons for Choosing Not to Become an IP

With these great things in store, why doesn't everyone make the trip to indispensability? There are reasons— some quite seductive—that might lead you, an otherwise ripe candidate for IP status, to say, "Thanks, but no thanks."

Mistaken Belief That Others Already See You as Indispensable

If you are a good worker, regularly receive excellent performance reports, and tend to be optimistic, you may privately discount the possibility that *you* might be ushered out as part of a corporate reshuffling, merger, or acquisition. The question here, of course, is whether your optimism is well founded.

Here is one perspective on the question of who goes and who stays. When senior managers decide that they must significantly reduce costs or choose between competing staff members in the wake of melding with another entity, three rough groupings emerge:

1. Those who are reputed to be difficult, disruptive, or deadwood. Of course, these unfortunates are seldom baldly told why they are so expendable. Why be candid about it, when they can be eased out as part of a "general reduction in staff"?

2. The highest valued, the indispensables. These are the people to be saved at all costs. They are quietly, even surreptitiously, asked to apply for

key jobs with assurance (at least as much assurance as contractual obligations will allow) that they will indeed get them.

3. Everyone else.

In a tiered layoff that takes place over a year or two, the most expendable will naturally go first. Those with the best technical skills will go last, but given a great enough appetite for cost cutting, even they will go. When the layoffs are massive, hurried, or the result of mergers, even these fine distinctions fall by the wayside, and all but the indispensables are turned loose by plant, by region, or by country. Clearly, the best way to fireproof yourself is to become identified as indispensable.

You can test whether you are already one of that number by asking your boss, "If we're faced with a massive layoff, will I be one of those who is retained?" If the response is equivocation, irritation, or a weaselly "Don't worry about it, you're doing fine," you'll know you have work to do.

Time and Effort

Recasting yourself as an indispensable person will require a commitment of time and effort on top of everything else on your plate. There is no effortless way to readjust habitual ways of thinking or learn new skills. Yes, the IP attributes you'll acquire or polish will help you to accomplish more with less strain, but unless you're already committed to unremitting self-development (in which case you may already be an IP), you might be reluctant to undertake an added load—that is, until the layoff is already on the horizon. Then, of course, it may be too late.

Discomfort at Being Different

It can be uncomfortable to believe that friends and colleagues see you as a pretentious glory seeker, no longer just one of the crowd. Although this may not be true in fact, perceptions can become the reality.

Lee Garry, a newly appointed regional marketing manager, decided to fully develop all his quite substantial abilities. As part of that effort, he arranged to be one of my coaching clients. The only one of his groups to have embarked on such a program, he was appalled to discover that his colleagues resented his earnest recountings of his learning adventures. When the kidding at their monthly meetings began to take on an edge and one of them pointedly asked if he weren't "going too far with this onward and upward stuff," he began to slack off.

Without a conscious decision to bail out of his program entirely, Lee canceled several of our consultations. Then, earnestly denying that he had given up on his development, he nevertheless told me that he was "just too busy right now."

Risk of Being Disliked

It shouldn't surprise you that indispensable people are not universally liked. While most coworkers value them—after all, IPs are helpful, at least when it's needed, and add much to the success of the enterprise—there are exceptions. For example, wanna-be IPs, who drudge away for long hours and otherwise struggle to please their bosses, are understandably jealous of those who are what the wanna-bes wish to be. Similarly, insecure bosses can sometimes resent those who have contributed most to their success. When that resentment leads to unpleasantness or career blockage, IPs simply resign, often to work for a competitor, a sort of poetic justice.

Making the Commitment

Mike Geber, the engineering manager we introduced in Chapter 3, struggled with making a commitment to becoming an IP. It was not just the added workload that most bothered Mike; he resented the need to change himself simply to remain employable. "I've done pretty well up till now," he said, "and the corporate hacks I've run into are not such great shakes themselves. It's not as if I haven't done a lot already. I've been promoted twice since I've been here. When I was good enough before, why am I not good enough now?"

Like Mike, you may feel that the entire notion of trying to make yourself over into an indispensable person is denigrating, as if you were not already a person of some considerable worth. If so, remind yourself that you're undertaking this chore for your own reasons; it was not imposed on you. Even if your interest was piqued by some disagreeable event on the horizon, you do always have another alternative: do nothing and wait for events to overtake you. After all, there's a fair chance you'll survive *this* layoff.

On the other hand, you may be feeling tired in advance without cause. You might not have all that much to do to boost yourself from the category of contributing but expendable employees to the category of indispensable people. After all, you're not trying to reconstruct your basic personality, just pick up the key indispensable attributes you don't already have. So, before you either commit yourself to becoming an indispensable person or decide it's not for you, take the time to identify which qualities you'll need to develop by matching yourself against the core attributes of indispensability. To do this, you need to be aware of the more subtle ways in which we all deceive ourselves about ourselves.

Don't Fool Yourself

To see yourself objectively is difficult; your protective ego sees to that. You can counter much of the obfuscation, however, if you know in advance what to expect.

We Create Ourselves for Ourselves

There is overwhelming evidence—as if we needed it—that our feelings, wishes, and desires profoundly influence the way we see our world, including that part of it we call ourselves. In a very real way, we tell stories about ourselves to ourselves, rather than merely recording what's actually going on. Having perceived things in a way that keeps our pictures of ourselves intact, we then diligently apply our crafty intelligence to the task of rendering our distortions plausible. It's easy to see why the brightest people seem so out of touch with the person others see.

The Strength-Weakness Paradox

Liabilities are nothing more than strengths inappropriately or excessively applied. Let's say you see yourself as steadfast, gritty, and unwaveringly persistent. You are therefore justifiably surprised when an exasperated colleague accuses you of being inflexible or rigid. Yet "rigid" and "steadfastly persistent" are, in fact, simply two manifestations of the quality of maintaining one's position in the face of contrary forces. There is a difference, but it is primarily one of degree.

The notion that too much of a good thing can create problems is certainly not new. Moreover, recent studies of decision making and interpersonal influence have helped to specify just how and why competent people misapply their best qualities to achieve the worst results. Take the quality of aggressiveness, just what is needed to make someone active and forceful, a real go-getter, the confident producer of results. That same desirable quality, used excessively, turns "active" into "pushy," forcefulness into bullying, and "go-getter," into "empire builder." Often the behavioral distance between just enough and too much is rather small—an added reason why your evaluation of yourself might differ from another's. It's easy to see how Mike Geber's bosses could see him quite differently than he saw himself.

While sitting in on one of Mike's departmental meetings, I heard him coherently and with enthusiasm present to his staff a new series of product initiatives. Halfway through the meeting, someone raised a rather minor objection—at least it so seemed to me—prompting Mike to scathingly lecture the unfortunate source of that "resistance" on why the concerns that had prompted her questions had no merit. Clearly, he was both the assertive and enthusiastic leader that he saw himself as *and* the contentious, overreaching egotist who at some earlier time had offended an influential senior manager.

From the Inside, Things Look Different

To further complicate matters, most of us don't give much thought to the possibility that we might be judging ourselves against criteria quite different from those held by others who are important to the success of our work. For Mike, units out the door and low warranty costs were the measures of managerial performance that counted, far outweighing his coworkers' occasional hurt feelings. He was certainly correct that his bosses were mightily pleased by high production figures, but he erred in assuming that they did not hold interpersonal skills equally important, especially for a possible promotional candidate. It's not hard to see why he saw himself as highly competent, a most valued employee, when, in fact, he was high on the list for the first round of downsizing separations.

Adding to the confusion is the likelihood that, while you will see your behavior as a reasonable response to what's happening around you, your associates will tend to interpret your behavior as a result of *who* you are, often thinking about it as "just like Mike." Of course, both perspectives are to some extent correct. What you do at any given time is affected both by the requirements of the situation and by your tendency to act consistently across all situations. If being objective about yourself means seeing yourself as others see you, the task can be difficult, just because you and they may focus on different sides of this equation.

Finally, as an intelligent human being, while not particularly intending to, you have acquired a repertoire of fancy techniques that help you to see yourself in the best light possible.

I Didn't Do It, and If I Did, It's Not My Fault

We all have ideal images of ourselves—the person we would like to be or at least think we should be. Sure, your image is constantly jarred—when you are caught in a mistake, say, or glance at an uncomplimentary snapshot, forget an appointment, or turn in a less than ideal performance. But even in the face of such constant reminders of your imperfect humanity, your ideal self will continue to pummel you with standards that often are unrealistically high. It has a first-rate weapon for doing just that: it can make you feel anxious. When anything you do, think, or feel doesn't conform to your ideals, you get zapped—by a twinge in your diaphragm, a hurting head, a painfully tense back, or simply an awful feeling of impending disaster.

It's not surprising, therefore, that—as we all do—you have put into place two neat defenses against your ideal self's manhandling (actually, one defense with two faces): denial and blame. These wonderful defenders work either by impeaching the evidence that you're not all that you want, should, or expect to be, or by laying on others the blame for whatever went wrong. Some of the fancy sidestepping I have heard from intelligent and highly placed people ranges from simple denial ("I just don't do that") to those elaborate rationalizations sometimes referred to as "explaining it all away": "Yes, I do tend to argue hard, but I have a lot of important things to say, and anyway, since *I've* done my homework, I know when I'm right." All true, of course, but it is also true that the good ideas of those intimidated into silence were lost, and that few of those people are likely to cooperate well. Of course, when the project that you argued your colleagues into fails, you can always blame the incompetents who implemented it.

Correct Errors in Self-Perception

In the face of all this efficient obfuscation, how are you to gain a balanced, more or less objective picture of your present level of functioning? Two actions can help: observing yourself for a time and then checking out your observations with those who know you.

Observe Yourself in Action

Rather than depending solely on your recollection of how you typically function, take some time to simply observe yourself in action. Some people are more introspective than others, ruminating often about the whys of their behavior. If you tend toward such self-reflection, keeping an eye on yourself will simply be an extension of what you regularly do, except that now you'll focus more on *what* you say and do, rather than why in the world you've done it On the other hand, if you tend toward a more outgoing and action-oriented outlook—impatient with too much speculation over the whys and wherefores of your behavior—you may feel that time devoted to purposely observing yourself would be better spent on the real work that needs to be done. Even so, remind yourself that having a clear picture of what you need to do to make yourself indispensable is the efficient way to go.

Think of yourself as a behavioral scientist observing the most interesting of subjects: you. Listen to the sound of your voice in meetings and in your briefings with your boss. Although you've always thought of yourself as a team player, do you notice that you look busy when an overloaded teammate silently appeals for your help? Do you decide without getting broad feedback first? Do you find yourself in an "either it's my way or no way" argument when you should be searching for a mediated solution that gets at what both parties want? Mike Geber remained convinced that he was already an indispensable person—if only he could get others to see it—until he suddenly realized that he had prepared a complex interdepartmental project proposal without input from either his staff or the colleagues who would be contributing time and resources to its implementation. He even heard his "This is just a straw man for the next division staff meeting" as the rationalization it was.

You can add depth to your observations by attending carefully to thoughts that flit through your mind as you compare your current behavior to the indispensability criteria. Are you explaining away any discrepancies between what you do and what the most highly valued people do? ("I'm too busy to spend my time going around soliciting a hundred opinions on every decision.") Do you find yourself blaming the discrepancies on your colleagues or bosses? ("Why should I pay attention to my boss's problems when he doesn't seem to care about mine?") Let those defensive reactions cue you that you're uncomfortably aware that your present behavior doesn't yet match indispensability standards.

Check Out Your Observations with Others

To see yourself in a more well-rounded way, solicit feedback from your boss, coworkers, and spouse or partner. One way to help them articulate their impressions—credit Mike Geber, engineer that he is, for this method—is to list the ten attributes you're most interested in. (You can list them all if you wish, but your informants might be overwhelmed.) Ask them to rate you on a scale of one (meaning you don't do this much) to ten (you do this a lot). Tell your informants that you intend to use the information as part of a development plan for yourself, that you'd like their candid opinions, and that your feelings won't be hurt no matter how many low ratings show up. Don't be offended if they seem to emphasize your shortcomings and come up short about your positives. Like most people, they will have attended more to what about you bothered them and less to what they've appreciated. (This tendency is one source of that most common of subordinate complaints, "I never get enough positive feedback.")

Throughout all this soul-searching, buoy yourself with the knowledge that you'll gain more than encouragement from this assessment. Knowing yourself better in a specific rather than general way, and acknowledging that there are yet some things that even you can learn, are the first and perhaps the most important steps toward becoming a better version of yourself.

Estimate Which Attributes You Need to Develop

Having eyed yourself, heard about yourself from others, and noticed whichever kinds of denial are your specialty, you're now ready to estimate how much of each of the indispensable qualities described in Chapters 2 and 3 are already part of your repertoire. Read through the self-survey, taking plenty of time to consider each item separately. Mark the scale below each item to show how frequently each attribute is part of your current experience. Stay focused on what you actually do without regard for the reasons why you are, or are not, behaving that way at present.

Self-Survey: Your Indispensable Qualities

Qualities of Mind

1. I decide only after broad input.

To a very little extent	To a little extent	To some extent	To a great extent	To a very great extent
1	2	3	4	5	6	7

2. I search for and can discern underlying causes of problems.

To a very little extent	To a little extent	To some extent	To a great extent	To a very great extent
1	2	3	4	5	6	7

3. I avoid oversimplifying complex problems.

To a very little extent	To a little extent	To some extent	To a great extent	To a very great extent
1	2	3	4	5	6	7

4. I can see interconnections among seemingly diverse factors.

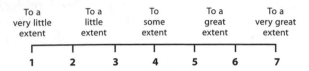

5. I can switch perspectives easily.

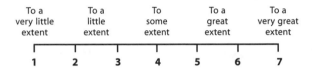

Organizational and Interpersonal Skills

6. I speak my mind directly but without attacking.

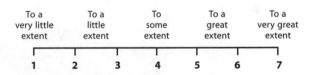

7. I am open to input from others.

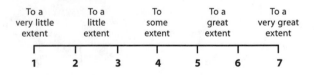

8. The way I am with others does not vary, regardless of their status or other attributes.

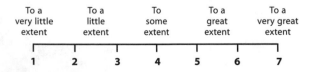

9. I am helpful to coworkers and others when the help is asked
    for and needed.

To a very little extent	To a little extent	To some extent	To a great extent	To a very great extent
1	2	3	4	5	6	7

10. I adjust well to change.

To a very little extent	To a little extent	To some extent	To a great extent	To a very great extent
1	2	3	4	5	6	7

11. I'm skillful at mediating disagreements toward win-win
    solutions.

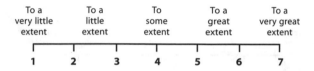

To a very little extent	To a little extent	To some extent	To a great extent	To a very great extent
1	2	3	4	5	6	7

12. I think and act as if I were an "owner."

To a very little extent	To a little extent	To some extent	To a great extent	To a very great extent
1	2	3	4	5	6	7

13. I don't compromise my personal standards.

To a very little extent	To a little extent	To some extent	To a great extent	To a very great extent
1	2	3	4	5	6	7

14. I respect organizational boundaries and roles (avoid turf wars, delegate well).

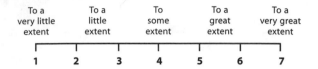

15. I have a positive, can-do outlook.

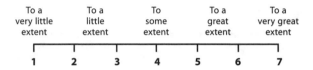

16. I react nondefensively to mistakes or criticism.

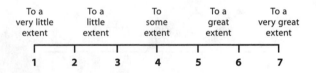

17. I'm an avid and continuous learner.

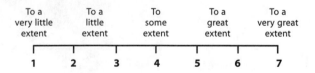

18. I maintain a satisfactory balance between my work and personal life.

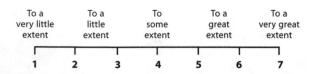

Having assessed how far along you are toward becoming an indispensable person, you're ready to commit yourself to a plan of action. Take plenty of time to think through what you hope to gain and what it will cost you. As a rule, the farther to the left you've placed your check marks, the more time and effort you will need to arrive at your goals. Remember, you're committing yourself to continued personal growth for the balance of your working life; this is one personal project for which a quick fix is just not possible. On the other hand, it is equally true that every step along the way will increase your value to your organization and will make you less dependent on the goodwill of anyone but yourself. Best of all, you'll feel extraordinarily good about yourself.

Having decided to continue, you are ready for planning how, when, and where to start your program—which is just what Chapter 5 is about.

5

Planning Your Indispensability Program

"I don't know whether I'm encouraged or discouraged," said a puzzled Mike Geber. He had just finished perusing his self-prepared indispensability survey. "Seven of the eighteen indispensable qualities look hopeless, five seem OK as is, and six are in the middle. Since we're still pretty much hierarchical around here, learning how to mediate disagreements is pretty irrelevant. Other than that, though, I can't see that any of them can be ignored. If everything I need to do is as much work as I think, I'll be retired before I become indispensable. It's just too much!"

"Well," I suggested, perhaps a bit fatuously, "maybe you need a plan."

"I know *that*, Doc, but what do I put in the plan?"

WHEN YOU ARE overwhelmed by the prospect of a challenging and complex task, the best strategy *is* to have a plan. One that tells you how and where to start, how to know when you've gotten to where you want to go, what to watch out for along the way—and, especially, a plan that enables you to tackle that daunting task one step at a time. Yes, it's true that sometimes planning can be become a substitute for action, but it's also true that planning—which is, after all, a kind of action—can be the first step to getting started. As a bonus, it will help you to make the best use of your time and energy.

For one thing, your plan, replete with steps to be followed, helpful hints, and even sketchy scripts, will help you to stay the course long enough for the new methods and approaches to become part of your ordinary repertoire. When you start to change a practice that has become habitual, you should expect to feel uncomfortable, as if the new way were "unnatural." Whether changing your grip on a tennis racket or mediating a disagreement you formerly would have resolved by edict, you might as well prepare for a protesting inner groan and an impulse to return to what feels right.

Your plan will also keep you headed toward the proper targets. Remember, the chief value of the indispensable-person template is that it focuses you on personal development that really counts in the employment marketplace. Similarly, your plan will enable you to zero in on the skills and attitudes that *you* need to modify, to avoid those that are either too much of an initial stretch or too inconsequential, and to decide which to tackle first. While it might be tempting to take on the whole array of indispensable qualities at once, the most likely result would be a little progress on many of them but not enough to really make a difference.

Finally, there is good evidence that commitments get stronger when you write them down, especially when you review them with another person. Converting intentions into written symbols not only makes them more concrete, but it becomes a first action step, increasing the likelihood that you will promote your commitment to make yourself indispensable from "should do it" to "will do it."

Your action plan should answer these questions:

- With which IP attributes will I start?

- What specifically do I need to change?

- Where can I get support?

- How will I know I've made progress?

- How will I acquire the methods, skills, or perspectives I'll need to become an IP?

After a week of wrestling with his first list of target attributes, Mike Geber handed me the list accompanied by the ensuing conversation. "Well, setting priorities and following them so I'm using my time efficiently is maybe my first goal. Boning up on the latest CAD/CAM software should pay off in solving engineering problems. And I suppose I ought to get better at passing on what I know in a way that doesn't turn off my coworkers up, down, and sideways. You know, I'm seen as coming on too strong sometimes."

"Sometimes?" I thought, but what I said was, "These all seem worthwhile, Mike, but how do you connect them with the list of IP attributes? For instance, I've heard that you are personally quite productive, which says to me that you must be handling priorities pretty well."

"Oh, the attributes," he said. "Well, I looked them over, figured I was already rather sharp at analyzing problems, but I had to admit that I usually decide on the basis of my own thinking."

"So one of your IP goals," I persisted, perhaps a bit impatiently, "is 'Decide' only after broad input."

He stared at me blankly for a few seconds, then grinned. " OK, I finally get it. I wasn't really thinking about those attributes of yours as a template, but more like a general call for upgrading myself. So your point is I might end up a sharper engineer with maybe a slightly broadened view of the world, but not much more indispensable than I was before. Have I got the message?"

"Mostly," I proffered, knowing it was not quite that simple but not wanting to quench his enthusiasm. "The advantage of focusing in on 'my attributes' is that you'll end up with what those who count have said they value the most."

The first step in developing your own plan is to sit with the list of IP attributes in front of you and decide where you'll start. Here are some rules of thumb that will help you select a realistic and achievable set of goals.

Not Too Few, Not Too Many

Much evidence indicates that successful developmental efforts are built around moderately difficult learning tasks, neither too easy nor too hard, neither too few nor too many. If you bite off too much to start—for example, you select more than seven IP attributes—your program may starve because enough time and attention can't be squeezed from your already too busy schedule, expire from an overdose of the unfamiliar, or simply peter out because no one but you is forcing you to become indispensable. On the other hand, fewer than three goals may stretch out the time it takes to make significant progress beyond the onset of your next layoff crisis.

As you ponder whither and whether you're going, stay alert for a temptation to dismiss the whole thing as silly nonsense. Remind yourself of the road hazards to well-intentioned development plans that we covered in Chapter 4, and keep on with your planning.

Start Where You're Most Comfortable

You can minimize any hesitant feelings about this undertaking by starting with the attributes that are the most compatible with your present outlook and repertoire of skills. By beginning your program with qualities that already fit well with your style, you won't have to do much in the way of a radical reconfiguration of your personality. Don't fret about being too easy on yourself, because there is an attitudinal component to just about any significant behavioral change.

Let's say that you've decided to acquire more of the "helpful mentor" quality that characterizes most IPs. On the face of it, you only need a commitment to be more helpful, but beneath the surface there may be more. For example, if you care about how well you stack up against others, an overheard compliment given to one of your peers can provoke an immediate, but subtle, flick of anxiety. Later, without quite knowing why, you'll respond negatively to the complimenter's (or the complimentee's) otherwise reasonable requests for help. Needless to say, you won't think of yourself as unhelpful but will expertly rationalize your unfriendly behavior—"too much to do" always works. Meanwhile, you'll have acquired the label of "unhelpful," never really understanding why. To move beyond that feeling of annoyance at being asked for help, you may need to do more than a little thinking through. In Chapters 6, 7, and 8, you'll find suggestions for managing the attitude change to become an IP.

Combine Learning Targets Whenever You Can

You can combine a number of the IP attributes into a single learning target, because the qualities are somewhat interconnected. For example, one way to "obtain broad input prior to deciding" is to appear "open to others." In addition to cutting your overall effort by one-eighteenth, combining learning targets can add interest to the learning of both parts. However, don't lose sight of the fact that the qualities are distinct. Obtaining input prior to a decision and appearing open to others both contribute to the aura of indispensability.

Choose Qualities Important to Your Job and Organization

Other things being equal, you might as well select IP qualities that are most relevant to your job and seen as important by the decision makers in your organization. Your present bosses can be helpful in working this out if they are in step with where the organization is going. If not, they may not be as indispensable as you hope to be, so they may not be in place when decisions about your fate come along.

Take George Semple, Mike Geber's boss's boss, as a good example of how that can happen. George had been a division general manger for seven years and was highly valued because of his analytically plotted plans, tight budgets, and cautious approach to implementation. (It's easy to see why Mike's slam-bang aggressive approach often offended him.) There was certainly strength in his careful management style, and over the years his division had prospered—until surging competition and a shifting customer base brought a new CEO. George carried on as usual (after all, the right way to do things was the right way to do things), unmoved by the blatherings of others that corporate survival needed team players who could quickly package innovative products to meet changing market conditions. Was George immediately let go to open the way for a more flexible integrative type? Not at all. He had served long and well and, more to the point, was a personal friend of corporate senior managers, who could see little reason to create an emotional hassle when George would shortly be restructured out anyway. That is exactly what happened a year later.

Until then, of course, Mike had to continue to provide George with the careful analyses he wanted. But it also became clear to Mike that his own IP targets ought to be those that would increase his value as a broad-gauged and flexible gatherer of resources. For example, he would need to improve his skill at mediating disagreements among team members without eroding their enthusiasm.

Start with Qualities That Others Will Notice

Becoming a totally indispensable person might take more time than your corporate restructuring will allow. Therefore, select learning targets that make the most difference in how you're seen by those who will make the layoff decisions. For example, acquiring the knack for relating to senior managers as equals will set you apart from most others as a solid person of strength and presence. On the other hand, improving your ability to discern the underlying causes of problems, while of immense value, is not likely to be noticed out of hand. Unfortunately, the state of the world is such that you must not only *become* an indispensable person, but you must look like one.

In the same vein, don't allow your enthusiasm to induce you to expand your plan from a limited set of indispensable attributes to a broadly based plan for general development. While highly desirable as an end in itself, becoming a better person or more proficient at your trade will not make you look like an indispensable person. Once again, the value of knowing what real indispensable people are like enables you to fashion learning goals that are not only concrete and specific but to the point.

After sitting with these notions for a week, Mike revised his indispensable target list, resulting in five goals:

1. Learn to mediate disagreements toward win-win solutions.

2. Decide only after broad input.

3. Be open to input from others.

4. Maintain a positive, can-do outlook.

5. Respect roles and boundaries (so I won't look like an empire builder).

Was Mike really starting with the attributes most important to his quest? Perhaps not, but simply getting started in a way that made sense to him was far more important than having selected exactly the right mix. Perhaps he was confusing his clever use of the hyperlogical, formula-driven approach he had learned in engineering school with the more intuitive feel for underlying systems that characterizes most IPs. But if he pays attention to others' input and learns how to mediate disagreements, he may come to see that logic and intuition are both powerful tools for understanding. He can learn more about how to think like an IP later.

Deciding What Specifically to Change

Having decided just which attributes to acquire, your next step is to turn each attribute into a specific learning target. While your first thought might have been "What targets? All I need to do is be 'open to input,'" your second thought, we hope, was "However one does that." In other words, you need to convert a general goal (such as being open to inputs) into specific and achievable learning activities (the ways you will learn to be open).

Doing that may take some thinking. Start by jotting down just what has kept you from acting as you've decided you want to act. For example, think about what has prevented you from being open to input from others. Then challenge each of your "reasons" to clarify just what attitudes or skills you'll need to modify or acquire. Your list of reasons, and accompanying challenges, might look something like Mike's, shown in the table.

Sample Self-Analysis for Setting Learning Targets

Desired Attributes
Being open to input from others

Reasons for Not Changing	Challenges to Reasons
I don't really believe that getting everyone's input is what a strong-minded manager does.	Maybe that's one reason why I'm seen as being pushy. Do I choose to stand pat with that attitude or try to modify it?
I'm overloaded already; I can't take the time to listen to everyone's ideas.	Do I need to differentiate between key decisions, for which I'll force the time to obtain broad input, and most others, which I still ought to make on my own?

If I already know what the score is, why waste time asking others?	Do I believe that others' ideas are never useful?
	    Am I closing off my thinking too soon?
	    Maybe I just need to learn how to integrate opinions that differ from my own.

I get impatient when others go on too long.	Do I understand what cues trigger my impatience?

Learning Targets

- I need to change my thinking so that I believe that others have something worthwhile to say.

- I need to learn techniques for putting others at ease and prompting them to talk.

- I need to learn what I do that tends to turn others off. Do I interrupt them, finish their sentences for them, look impatient when they seem to go on too long?

Having put yourself through this sometimes eye-opening exercise, your next step will be to make some guesses about what has to happen inside you in order to make your desired attribute truly descriptive of you. For example, what changes in your thinking, feeling, or behavior will be necessary for you to become open to input from others? At the bottom of the table are three of Mike Geber's conclusions about how he had to change if he were to become more open.

> When Mike sat down with me to review his learning targets, he was genuinely puzzled. "Is this all there is to it? I decide that I'm going to suddenly be interested in what other people have to say, even though I *know* that I get antsy when they're telling me things I already know? How do I change what I believe if I believe it? And I've already had 'active listening' in my basic management course, but I'm still not much of a listener. Most of all, how do I stop offending people—at least that's the

message I get from our division's human resources manager—when I'm not even sure what I do that pisses
them off? I need some help here, Doc."

Is simply deciding to become an indispensable person all that you need to do, or will you have to do some
mind bending to start thinking like an IP? What about
the behavioral flaws you've picked up? Do they need
to be overcome? And, if so, how? These are pivotal
questions, key to the whole enterprise of remaking your
working self to become indispensable. Fortunately, there
are some optimistic answers to each of them.

Is Deciding to Become an IP Enough?

On the surface, it may seem naive to believe that simply deciding to become indispensable won't be just one
more desired remake that will lead to more guilt than
changed behavior. After all, there is ample evidence
that simply wanting to change—to spend more time
with our families, to gain weight, to lose weight, to
give up a satisfying but harmful habit—is seldom suf-
ficient. On the other hand, people do change all the
time, even when it's tough to do. About half of all
paroled criminals go straight, many addicts stay in
recovery, some terrible-tempered bosses eventually
reform, and a few of us are even able to adjust our eat-
ing habits to maintain a desirable weight. Understanding the why of these differences can help you in
your own transformation into an indispensable person.

What Conditions Us to Change

Whether you're going to change for the better or the worse depends largely on how you resolve the tangled equation of often conflicting impulses, desires, fears, and injunctions that are every human being's inheritance. Suppose we ask you to tell us about yourself, and you feel inclined to do so. You'll first describe what it's like to be you, how it feels, what you want or don't want, and—perhaps after a little coaxing—what leaves you uncomfortable or fearful. If we probe a little further, you may also tell us how you would like to be, the kind of person you wish you were. Then—perhaps a bit ruefully—you'll recite the myriad rules for proper living that were poured into you by your parents and other adults to define the person others expect you to be. Your description thus encompasses an inner cast of three characters:

1. You as you experience yourself—confident but also harboring a few fears and doubts

2. Your ideal self—the indispensable, highly regarded person you want to be

3. A "should" self—a judgmental goad that subliminally whispers, "Don't let 'em push you around," or, "You always ought to help others"

How well these separate aspects of your self mesh largely determines whether you can do personal remodeling with relative ease or, conversely, why you sometimes need a stronger and more sustained commitment.

For example, if you have bought the notion that becoming an indispensable person is right for your career, that it's what a person with the right stuff—

however you define "right stuff"—would do, if you feel confident that you know how to become indispensable, in short, if your internal selves are all aligned, you can transform yourself with relative ease. Ease doesn't mean effortless—what meritorious goal is? You'll still need to choose a handful of attributes on which to start, think through what they'll require from you, acquire additional skills, and pay attention to what you're doing, until the new behaviors begin to feel natural. However, you will be ready for that sort of work—actually, it's the fun part—without having to realign any motivational innards.

When You Have to Modify Attitudes or Behavioral Flaws

The previous scenario was generally optimistic: You've always been an indispensable person inside, and you only need more explicit ideas on how to translate your inner inclinations into action. But for many people, the path to indispensability is a tougher climb. Many people's conception of a good person, employee, or manager doesn't quite jibe with key elements of the indispensable role. For example, Mike Geber wanted to be open to others, but openness didn't jibe with his sense of how a strong (decisive, independent, competitive, realistic) person ought to behave. Furthermore, many people feel resistance toward the idea of changing their ways "just to become more valued by an organization that doesn't care much about me." People in these situations have a little war going on inside themselves; they would like a solid way to deal with the turmoil of today's work world, but this route seems to pit their career aspirations against an important part of themselves. It doesn't take a clairvoyant to see that the most likely outcome would be lackadaisical learning, more than a little anguish, followed mercifully by the conclusion that there isn't any point to this whole business of becoming indispensable. To complicate matters even further, what if somewhere along the way you've picked up a difficult behavioral habit. Suppose you're seen as hardheaded or too soft a touch. You realize that, regardless of all your redeeming features, your particular flaw may set you up for "early retirement."

In any case, your first goal will be to modify the attitudes or behaviors that may limit your maximum self-fulfillment. How can you make these difficult changes? As usual, you have several alternatives. All are eminently doable, but they require inner sorting and relearning, some more than others. The best possibilities are: to emphasize the attributes that fit your personality as it is; reassess the validity of some of your conflicting "woulds," "coulds," and "shoulds"; and change a problematic attitude by behaving as if it had already changed.

The easiest way to get started is to shape the attributes that you need to acquire so they are aligned with important aspects of your self. For example, Mike Geber was stuck with an inner injunction that he should remain a "strong" person, so he learned how to "take charge" in the input-gathering processes that he instituted. Of course, he had to do it in a way that did not shut off just the conversation that he needed. Such realignments require a bit of ingenuity but are almost always possible.

A second, somewhat more laborious, approach is to modify whichever of your inner notions puts you in conflict with taking on an IP perspective. Thus, Mike might have dug into his belief that a bold person can't value others' opinions, a dogma likely acquired when he was too young to think rationally about it. He could have tested that belief in the light of his more adult perspective.

In many cases, what needs modifying is not a deep inner conviction. Rather, you may need to realign your habitual ways of behaving with perfectly satisfactory inner beliefs. It's easy to have that happen.

Charles Reilly, a highly competent member of his company's engineering research team, deeply believed that quality work, high standards, and teamwork—a favorite word of his—were essential to satisfying accomplishment. In practice, however (or so I was told by his fellow team members), he labored mightily just up to the edge of his own assignments. There he stopped and testily waited while his teammates caught up with him. If he had ideas that might have helped them—and he did; Charlie was very bright—he sat on them.

When I pointed out to Charlie that his behavior didn't fit with his oft-stated beliefs on the importance of teamwork, he corrected me by explaining that it was his teammates who were failing, not he. However, I noticed—as did his fellow researchers—that he henceforth began to take an interest in how they were doing, sat in on informal "skunk works," and rather nicely offered help when it was needed. Obviously, Charlie really did believe in teamwork; he simply didn't understand what teamwork required him to *do*. By focusing on your behaviors, attitudinal change will naturally follow.

How Can You Facilitate Change?

Once you start down your path to indispensability, you can facilitate transformation in several ways. Techniques that have helped many people include conversing with others about what you're trying to do, visualizing yourself as an indispensable person, and focusing your attention on process rather than outcome. Also, as we will discuss in the next section, identifying some friendly people to support you when the going gets tough is also very important.

Talk About What You're Trying to Do

There is increasing evidence that you can facilitate personal change by simply talking with interested listeners about how it's going. It's the kind of conversation fondly remembered by anyone lucky enough to have had a caring but realistic "Uncle Harry" or "Aunt Harriet" who would listen sympathetically to relationship, school, or career problems, with an occasional lifted eyebrow when emotion seemed to be overpowering good sense. Talk with yourself if no one else is available, but better, find others who will listen to what you're trying to do, what you're experiencing, and what you see happening as a result. We'll delve further into how to find those willing conversationalists when we look into building a support group later on in this chapter.

Visualize Yourself as an IP

Borrow an effective technique from the world of sports by occasionally visualizing yourself as an indispensable person. Build scenarios in your mind with you as hero or heroine, cleverly detecting underlying causes and hidden connections; listening intently to your staff, colleagues, or customers; giving avidly sought help; or taking responsibility for something amiss outside your own area. There is good evidence that visualization of this sort shortens learning time and shores up confidence in the face of new or unfamiliar challenges.

Focus on Process, Not Performance

While there are certainly advantages to setting goals and periodically monitoring how well you're achieving them, there is also ample evidence that when you concentrate too hard on the end of the chase, you'll perform less well and learn less from the experience. Many of us were mistakenly taught to focus on how well we are doing compared to our ultimate goals. However, you'll achieve more in the long run, achieve it more consistently, learn more, and gain more confidence from paying attention to precisely what you are currently doing and what that experience is teaching you. As Super Bowl–winning football coach Bill Walsh has put it, rather more dramatically, "When your goal is steady development rather than dramatic victories, the pieces fall into place in ways you can't initially predict."

If your goal is to become more able to see into problems, attend to how you're approaching the problem. Notice your immediate reaction when you started thinking about it, whether you're dismissing certain pathways, how you scan for targets of opportunity, and what specifically is most puzzling for you. In the long run—the important "run" when your goal is to become continually more indispensable—you will not only enhance your diagnostic problem-solving ability, but you'll solve more problems. Focusing on process rather than performance is probably the surest way to achieve that habit of mind—often cited but far less frequently exhibited—known as "working smart."

Building a Support Group

Carefully consider the possibility of enlisting others in your effort to become more well rounded, skillful, and indispensable. Possibilities for your support group might be your boss, subordinates, teammates, spouse, or close friends. You'll share with them your commitment to continuing development, mention the particular target behaviors you're trying to acquire, and use them for feedback on how well you're doing. Here are a few caveats to keep in mind as you go about assembling this cadre of supporters.

Soft-Pedal "Indispensability"

You may want to soft-pedal that you are working toward making yourself indispensable, or lighten up your statements with enough humor to avoid sounding either pompous or arrogant. Of course, you won't have to worry about this if you congregate with other budding indispensables—a definite plus, since they and you will constitute a ready-made conversation group. Talking about what each of you hopes to achieve and how well (or poorly) it's been going can accelerate the pace of everyone's learning.

Try Your Supervisor

Your supervisor, if he or she has opportunities to observe you in action, can be an excellent support person and certainly ought to be in favor of any work-related development. If, however, the indispensable qualities that you're pursuing seem not to fit with your supervisor's attitudes or perspectives—you are learning to see into the complex underpinnings of problems, but your boss is of a more black-and-white turn of mind—it's best to seek your support elsewhere.

Try Colleagues Outside Your Organization

If it's feasible, share your goals and why you're working toward them with collegial acquaintances outside your organization, perhaps those you've met through association activities or while attending professional conferences. The more you talk about these plans with others, the more concrete and "real" they will be to you. Who knows, your friends might decide to join you in the pilgrimage.

Brief Your Spouse and Significant Others

Share your plans, and the purposes behind them, with your spouse, family, or significant others. If they understand why you've committed more time and attention to your work life rather than to them, they can give you more support and encouragement in those moments of doubt that accompany any serious personal change.

Don't Be Sidetracked by Dogs in the Manger

Naturally, many of your colleagues will not be at all pleased to find that you have embarked on an organized effort to turn yourself into a most highly valued person. Their first response will likely be to talk you out of continuing with such foolishness. Expect to be told, "You don't need all that," "They have no right to ask that of you," "There's no such thing as an indispensable person," or any of the other great "truths" that have prevented most people from developing their full capacities. In the face of that kind of "help," thank the helpers for their interest and search for someone else with a more optimistic, can-do perspective on life.

How to Know if You're Making Progress

Every learning process has a beginning, a middle (replete with ups and downs), and no real end because there is never a limit to what can be learned. But there are points at which you might say, "I've now learned enough of x to satisfy my particular purpose." That's why graduation ceremonies are handy; they memorialize a midway achievement in an activity that could—and many say should—continue throughout your life.

When you're the only one in charge of your curriculum, you're the one who must decide when it's time to switch from one set of IP attributes to another. The time to consider just what will tell you that you've learned enough is before you start. Later on, your judgment may be clouded by those human tendencies toward self-delusion we touched on in Chapter 4.

To develop a set of "I've learned enough" indicators, ask yourself, "What will tell me that I'm using this new skill effectively?" Mike Geber has a list of answers to that question, and it looks like this:

- When I've learned to mediate disagreements, I will no longer arbitrarily decide who's right when my staff disagrees. I'll be using techniques I've learned in the "Resolving Conflicts" course I'm planning to take. My staff will comment on this (probably in shock).

- I'll know I've developed a broader view when I consistently canvass and *listen to* the ideas of my staff and colleagues before I finalize an important decision.

- I'll ascertain that I'm communicating better with staff and other directors by asking them privately about it. Most will tell me that I'm more open with them.

Although Mark's indicators left a lot to his ability to judge how others were responding to the changes he was intent on, he did describe a few *behaviors* that he hopes will have changed, and he included some outside checks. If all his indicators were in place six months later, we would undoubtedly be looking at a new Mike.

It's often not easy to describe in action terms just what will show that you've acquired a new perspective, but it's worth a try. Without some notion of what you'll be *doing* differently with a changed attitude, you can easily convince yourself that you have become "a more well-rounded person," without having changed your behavior much at all.

Choosing Methods, Techniques, and Perspectives

To complete your plan, you'll need to select the developmental activities that will move you toward your learning targets. For example, if you've decided you need to become better at putting others at ease and encouraging them to tell you what's really on their minds, you might (this time with serious intent) reread that old "learning to listen" manual or enroll yourself in a course on the same subject. You might also ask for feedback on your listening habits from someone you trust or simply alert yourself to notice how you communicate to others that you'd really rather not hear what they have to say.

Don't be surprised if you still feel some resistance to continuing on with this "silly" venture. The human mind is highly skilled at rationalizing the status quo: "After all, I've already read two books on the subject of listening, and if I really turned others off, I would have known about it long ago." Remind yourself that now you are *ready* to learn; before, you may not have been.

This part of your plan—which methods you'll start with, where and when you'll get going, what internal and external hindrances might prevent you from moving ahead, and how you'll deal with them—will be the real meat of your plan. Your next step is to move on to Chapters 6, 7, and 8, where you'll find exercises, suggestions, and helpful hints that will start you on your journey to acquire IP attributes.

Pointers for Building Your Repertoire of Indispensable Attributes

THE NEXT THREE chapters are designed to help you create your own unique program for becoming an indispensable person. You'll find a variety of methods, techniques, ideas, exercises, and cautions that have aided others to acquire the attributes we described in Chapters 1 through 3.

Chapter 6 suggests some approaches to gaining the breadth of view, systems orientation, and diagnostic skill that gain the respect of those who work with IPs. It also points out some common errors of perception and judgment that often creep into the thinking of the best of us. Make fewer of these stealers of mental effectiveness, and you will seem wiser and more soundly based than most.

Chapter 7 is a compendium of suggestions for gaining the most important interpersonal skills that marked our indispensable cadre: a knack for engendering trust; freedom from status tensions; communication that is candid but free from attack; helpfulness to others, within limits; and skill at mediating disagreements. You'll also find some tips on how to minimize or manage any problem behaviors that you may have picked up along the way.

Chapter 8 focuses on the indispensability aspects of work and the workplace: maintaining high personal standards; developing an owner's perspective; adapting easily to change; achieving a proactive, can-do attitude; and fostering a balanced life.

To make the best use of these chapters, be ready to jot down the methods or techniques that best fit your own plan for becoming an indispensable person. Supplement them with your own experience-gained ideas, and then start on your way to becoming truly "fireproof."

6

Thinking Like an Indispensable Person

INDISPENSABLE PEOPLE don't have higher IQs than their coworkers; they don't do better academically, aren't more expert in their fields, don't conceptualize more profoundly, and aren't particularly expert at the other qualities that most intelligence tests measure. But they do seem to use their intelligence particularly well, and perhaps as important, they misuse it less than others. More to the point, after years of insisting that "intelligence" was fixed at age fifteen, students of the mind have reached a new consensus that, with some effort, most of us can enhance our intellectual ability or at least learn to use what we have more effectively.

The suggestions in this chapter are based upon what researchers have learned about how to develop the following practical intelligence skills:

- Fitting the right style of thinking to the problems you encounter

- Stretching your mind for a broader outlook

- Avoiding oversimplification of complex problems

- Using a small-wins strategy

- Discerning interconnections and underlying causes

- Asking questions

- Prioritizing as much as you can

- Avoiding common errors in perception and judgment

Fitting the Right Style of Thinking to the Problems You Encounter

Most of us don't think much about how we think, so people are often surprised to discover that there is an impressive array of evidence that people differ in the ways they think about things. Each thinking style has its own set of powerful cognitive tools, as well as a tagalong assortment of blind spots and liabilities, most of which result from applying a perfectly useful way of thinking to the wrong problem, in the wrong way, at the wrong time. At times careful calculation and the application of a tried-and-true method is the thing, in other situations an intuitive, seat-of-the-pants decision is best, and in still others the problem will only open up to conceptualizing, even rank speculation.

The trick is to learn which style to use when, to find the right scalpel with which to cut through to the heart of any particular problem. But, in our investigations of managerial thinking styles and their relation to individual effectiveness, we've found that most people (85 percent) tend to consistently use one or two of the five styles we've identified, regardless of the nature of the problems with which they're faced. Interestingly, about 15 percent use all five styles about equally. Based upon our consulting experience with them, indispensable people fall into this latter group. So one way to think more like an IP is to extend your use of the styles that are your least favored, while staying alert to signs that you are pushing too hard on those you prefer. To do that, you'll need to recognize the five styles and know the main strengths and liabilities of each.

Five Styles of Thinking

The names we have given to the five styles of thinking are Synthesist, Idealist, Pragmatist, Analyst, and Realist. These names are descriptive of the thinking process rather than the person. As you read through the brief descriptions that follow, keep in mind that they seem to imply that a "Synthesist" thinker is solely guided by that style of thinking. In reality, we have all learned to use the thinking strategies that characterize the other styles to some extent. (That's why we all have the ability, although we may not always use it, to fit our style to the situation.) However, most of us prefer to use one or two of the five styles of thinking. Thus a person might think like a Synthesist most of the time but occasionally think like a Realist, Idealist, and so on.

Take a few moments to place yourself in one or two of the following categories of thinking styles. Since most people use a little of each style, you may see some of yourself in every category. Nevertheless, one or two styles should seem to fit you better than others. (If you would like further information on thinking styles, how they're measured, and how to use them for self-improvement, training, or team building, contact InQ Educational Materials, listed in the References at the end of this book.)

Synthesists

Synthesists are creative thinkers who have contradictory minds. When you say black, they think white; when you say long, they think short. They are intrigued by that which is different, unique, or complex, believing that the best solutions to problems emerge from the clash of conflicting views. Their minds are alert to underlying or even paradoxical connections that might shed light on the nature of the complexity. They ask "what if" questions that provoke abstract and argumentative discussions, sounding at times as if facts were of little consequence—much to the irritation of Realist thinkers, who believe that facts speak for themselves. For a Synthesist, however, the inferences one derives from those facts are the basis for construing reality.

Synthesists are not always more creative than others, but their speculative twists and turns often result in unusual and original perspectives. Most of the great

leaps in science have been the result of Synthesist thinking. As team members, they contribute by pushing their
colleagues to move beyond the surface agreements and
"obvious" assumptions that often oversimplify an issue.
In this way, Synthesists help the team—albeit reluc-
tantly—to avoid the perils of "groupthink." They are
at their best in research settings and in other complex
situations in which no clear path to a solution is evident and where issues and assumptions need to be identified and seen from all sides.

On the liability side, Synthesists can seem endlessly argumentative and may insist on surfacing every
issue, even when the matter is relatively trivial. Since
their thinking tends to have a "branching off" quality, moving laterally from topic A to topic Q, they
sometimes lose their more linear-thinking listeners.
Since speculation, newness, and complexity are what
interests them, Synthesists can become quickly bored
with everyday work routines, leaving such mundane
matters to others.

Idealists

For Idealists, reality is a unity into which new information is fitted in terms of its similarity to things
already known. Idealists have receptive minds, open
to any sort of input that will help them to a broader
understanding of the situation. Unlike Synthesists,
whose attention is caught by conflicts and contradic-
tions, an Idealist's focus is on the common ground that
is shared by all. Perhaps because of their concern for
the general welfare, Idealists care about long-range
impact. They ask, "For what good purpose are we
doing this?" and thus irritate their more success-
oriented colleagues.

Idealists' personal standards are high. Since these standards cannot always be met, they often feel disappointed in themselves for not living up to their own ideals, and in others—especially those who short-change, fudge on quality, or display flexible ethics. Thus, they are often depressed by much of what goes on around them. Idealist thinkers are at their best when there is a need for broad input, a long-range view, and a focus on goals and quality standards.

In hopes of meeting everyone's needs, Idealists often plan programs too broadly and set goals that are unrealistically high. They then may further decrease the possibility of success by screening out "hard" facts, such as budget overruns or the need for cost constraints. Receptive to many viewpoints, they may take too long to make a decision, trying to fit everyone's wishes into an ideal solution. Thus to Analyst and Realist thinkers, Idealists often appear overly sentimental and too worried about the impact of plans and projects on other people.

Pragmatists

In general, Pragmatists are adaptive thinkers. For them, *any* step that moves things along is acceptable. If this way won't do, they'll go that way, making whatever use they can of what they find. Unlike Analysts, who need to be convinced that a new way has merit, Pragmatists have more flexible minds, willing to let go of one idea if another seems worth trying. Since workability, rather than correctness, is their litmus test, they are freer to try a wide range of theories, plans, or procedures. They have little stake in proving that their own, or anyone else's, ideas are right. This flexibility of mind coupled with a belief that *any* step forward is worthwhile, makes Pragmatists see compromise as the best resolution when they run into resistance.

Rather than creating new perspectives, Pragmatists are more often known for finding new applications for old ideas, as well as quicker or easier ways to get jobs done. Their coworkers often describe them as resourceful or innovative. Probably as a by-product of their ability to switch perspectives quickly, Pragmatists are astute at sensing what will appeal to others, that is, what others want rather than what they need—a handy trait when selling is in the wind. In sum, the Pragmatist approach is most useful in situations that call for adaptability to changing conditions, where a long-range or systematic approach is not feasible, and where getting started, with small steps, is the best way to make progress.

Pragmatists' liabilities are best seen through the eyes of others. They often annoy Analysts with their seeming disregard for detailed plans and their casual way of floating along with any change in the prevailing current. At times, they offend Idealists because they seem willing to sacrifice high standards and consistency of purpose for the sake of an immediate gain. For Realist thinkers, a Pragmatist's penchant for compromise seems a show of weakness rather than wisdom.

Analysts

To an Analyst thinker, there is a best way to do just about anything. It will always be found by assembling data, ordering the data, and then applying logic and deduction until both the nature of the problem and its solution are nailed down. That which cannot be ordered, measured, or calculated lacks any real weight and can be safely ignored. It's the kind of thinking that has built every building, bridge, and other massive structure, and it has usually built them to last.

This deep belief in the power of rationality makes Analysts relatively immune to impulsive or emotionally driven actions, and others often see them as exceedingly strong-minded. Analysts are at their best in situations that require patience and perseverance, thorough attention to detail, and the cautious application of deductive logic to decision making.

When Analysts inappropriately apply their thinking, it can lead them to neglect those aspects of reality that cannot be easily quantified, including public fads and fancies, individual or cultural biases, intuitive or speculative ideas, customer whims, or employee spirit and morale. They may not plan well for contingencies, particularly those that arise from human unpredictability. Analyst thinkers are often accused of obsessive nit-picking and "paralysis by analysis," especially by impatient Pragmatists and Realists, who want to get started on plan A, which may be good enough, without waiting for all the i's to be dotted or for a careful analysis of the comparative merits of plans B, C, and D. Idealists often see Analysts as cold and insensitive to others' feelings.

Realists

The Realist's orientation is empirical and inductive; what can be seen, felt, heard, and experienced is what the world is all about. Because such directly experienced "facts" seem self-evident, Realists assume that everyone perceives and understands them in the same way, so they are not subject to disagreement. Realists' sureness that they are correct in what they believe gives them confidence to drive into action in the face of doubt and confusion, searching out whatever facts are available to direct observation and testing possible solutions against their own direct experience.

Because of their emphasis on execution and visible results, Realists often push passive or equivocating groups into action. They are at their best when there is a need for objectivity, drive, and risk taking, and for a rapid-fire and empirical approach to problem solving. Like Analysts, they are dubious about anything that seems unduly subjective or theoretical, usefully pushing others to be concise and to the point, and requiring them to validate their notions against the facts of immediate experience. Because they favor action over research, Realists often make good use of expert opinion. (You qualify yourself as an expert to a Realist by telling her something that her senses have already told her is true.)

As with the other styles, Realist liabilities stem from too much of an essentially useful quality. They will disparage Synthesist speculations even when an imaginative approach is exactly what is needed, and they sneer at the "bean counting" of Analysts when careful analysis might save costly overruns. From this perspective, the frequently observed conflicts among research staffs (often Synthesists), financial managers (often Analysts), and line executives (often Realists) seem almost inevitable, as well as unproductive. Idealists, who want to listen to every voice, fare little better. Realists write them off as overly sentimental, befuddled, indecisive, and worthy only of disregard. When Pragmatists advise sidestepping barriers or com-

promising for what is possible, their Realist colleagues—sure in their rightness—push them aside and
break through the barriers, sometimes also breaking
themselves. They tend to be uncomfortable with ambi-
guity and complexity and often urge, "Let's get the
show on the road," even when caution might serve
their purposes better. Realists are honestly baffled by
disagreement, often interpreting it as stupidity or resistance to be ignored or simply brushed aside. Consequently, others—especially subordinates—often see
them as railroading their ideas through.

How to Make the Most of Your Thinking Style

An understanding of the different ways that human
beings think has proved to have many useful applications. Three are particularly relevant to this brief look
at developing your capacity to think more like an indispensable person: deciding *how* to think about non-
routine problems, stretching yourself to think in
unfamiliar ways, and using the thinking styles of others to compensate for your blind spots.

Fit the Style to the Problem

If you apply the style of thinking that best fits the issue
at hand, your problem solving will be more pointed
and powerful. For example, think like an Analyst when
faced with budgetary and engineering problems, like a
Synthesist when a new or unusual marketing approach
is called for, like an Idealist when developing a mission statement or corporate strategy, and like a Prag-

> To get a feel for the power of this notion, imagine an emergency room physician waiting until all the appropriate tests have been run, and the best procedures thoroughly planned, before taking action. Although that scenario may seem far-fetched, I consulted with a physician client who loved the idea of emergency medicine but found that his Analyst approach ill equipped him for the rough-and-tumble of an emergency room.

matist or Realist when out in the field and forced to deal with an emergency system breakdown.

Stretch Your Mind a Bit

Press yourself to utilize thinking styles that are not your most preferred. A simple and straightforward tool for doing so is to keep handy the set of questions listed in the following table. They can induce you to consider a problem from the perspective of each of the five styles of thinking.

The technique is simple: When you face a problem of importance, take the time to apply each of the questions to that problem, especially noting the initial responses that flit through your mind, however irrelevant or silly. Think of them as clues to an aspect of the problem that your old habits of mind would have overlooked or ignored. Remember, you're trying to broaden your perspective and open yourself to unaccustomed ways of thinking.

Questions That Stretch Your Mind

Synthesist Questions

- What if (it were called . . . ; we did . . . ; they did . . .)?

- What are the essential differences among our alternatives?

- What are we assuming or taking for granted?

- What are alternate interpretations of what we're absolutely sure of?

- What would be the exact opposite of our present approach? (This is especially useful when a problem has resisted solution.)

Idealist Questions

- What past experiences is this similar to?

- How would other stakeholders view this situation?

- What would everyone, even our opposition, agree about?

- What if we kept on this route for the next five years?

- What projected actions would we be reluctant to reveal to our children or others who believe in us?

Pragmatist Questions

- What else can we do with it? (How else can we use these resources?)

- What compromises could we live with?

- How can we accumulate enough resources to get started?

- What small step would have the most leverage on the circumstances with which we have to contend?

- What's the best way to sell this? Why would anyone want to buy it?

Analyst Questions

- What would a model solution look like?

- What data do we have? What do we need?

- What would logic, divorced from emotion, tell us to do?

- How can we research this?

- What are the bare essentials we need to get the basic job done?

Realist Questions

- What resources do we need? Where can we get them?

- What actually happened?

- What are our action options?

- What feels right?

- Who are the experts in this?

Use Others' Thinking Styles to Fill in Your Gaps

When working on an important decision, obtain input from those who think differently than you. Force yourself to listen to what they have to say without comment, taking notes and making sure you understand their reasons for saying what they do. When reviewing your notes, ignore whether their comments were well taken or "right." Instead, concentrate on what they seem to be after; perhaps their aims are worthwhile and you can find a way to achieve them. Consider any objections to your plan as contingencies that need attention before you implement it.

Also, consider using "novices"—support staff members, friends, spouse, or partner—to help you see flaws that your "expertise" has masked. Knowing too much about any subject can prevent you from seeing it in a novel perspective. While using tried-and-true methods is efficient, those habitual responses can induce you to overlook situational differences that might call for a different approach.

Avoid, for as long as possible, explaining your own proposed solutions to others. There is much evidence that as you explain a course of action, you further convince yourself that it's the only possible way to go. Wait until you've fully examined the problem from all sides.

Avoiding Oversimplification of Complex Problems

Although we should know better, most of us hate to face the reality that neat solutions seldom solve messy problems. Perhaps we resist this idea because simple answers to complex questions are so comforting. They enable us to dodge the reality that we can't or won't invest the resources that a more realistic assessment might force upon us, so we feel better—for a while. Also, when we posit an optimistic, if simpleminded, way of dealing with a problem, we can sell it more easily than a multifaceted solution that deals with all of the complexity. "We cut staff by 10 percent because increased competition forces us to reduce costs," if firmly enough said, forecloses disagreeable questions, and it contains enough truth to leave the impression that cutting personnel will indeed put us ahead of our competition.

Actually, our early experiences have taught most of us to expect and be satisfied with oversimplifications.

A query like "Why can't I have ice cream before dinner?" evoked a simple answer: "Because it will spoil your appetite." Neither we, nor our grown-ups, really wanted to undertake dealing with the complexity of a more complete response: ". . . and my mother never let *me* have ice cream before dinner, and if *I'm* on a diet, it's not fair for you to enjoy ice cream, and I already feel enough guilt about whether I'm a proper parent, and who's in charge around here anyway," and so on ad infinitum. Finally, some minds are more comfortable with black-or-white assessments, feeling that shades of gray are for sissies. Recall those hardheaded Realists and strong-minded Analysts, who often take the lead when decisions are made.

Symptoms of Oversimplification

To avoid oversimplifying, identify and then watch out for the thoughts, feelings, and telltale phrases that signify you may be sliding into simplifying when you should be sorting out complexity. Examples might be a feeling of frustration when an associate continues to blather on about a problem to which you're certain you have a solution, and those comforting but limiting thoughts such as "All I have to do is . . . ," or "All that's wrong is . . . ." Once you've alerted yourself to the possibility that you've unconsciously put your brain in neutral, reengage by saying something on the order of, "But let's take another look at it."

When you are problem solving in a group, be alert to a transition from a search for the best (most comprehensive, long-lasting, etc.) solution to an either/or argument: "It's either raise prices or fire employees."

Not only does a polarized conversation narrow the focus to choosing one of two alternatives—each of which only partly engages the whole of the issue—but the emotionality generated by the fight will narrow the participants' sights still further. The "winning solution" will have simplistically done away with the projected positives of the "loser"; when implemented, it will achieve only partial success, all that is possible.

To prevent oversimplification, try some version of "We seem to be arguing. In my experience there is usually some 'right' on both sides." Then mention that decision-making experts all point out that the correct way to deal with a discussion that has polarized is to change the question from "Should we go north or south?" to "How do we achieve the benefits that we would have obtained from going north *and* from going south?"

Don't be offended if the group either ignores your first attempts to move beyond argument or becomes annoyed. Arguing may not be constructive, but it can be fun. However, if you persist with "This sounds like an either/or argument," the reasonableness of your effort should finally prevail.

Using a Small-Wins Strategy

To make headway in a complex situation, adopt a small-wins strategy. The *small* in a small-wins strategy doesn't imply trivial, nor does it mean giving up on an important yet hard-to-reach goal. This strategy is, rather, a way of making progress through a complex problem situation when you're not yet sure what a comprehensive solution might be. You simply tackle your hard-to-reach goal one step at a time, and each step is a small win.

Let's say you are the training manager in a medium-sized company, and you would like a promotion to the director level. A simplified definition of the problem might be "All I need is to be dependable, get along well with my staff and colleagues, and show that I have leadership ability." While that definition of the problem is certainly virtuous, it doesn't seem quite in touch with such complexities as a perennially tight budget, able competitors for scarce promotions, the personal favoritism of senior managers (many of whom you do not know well), and other deplorable realities of organizational life. An open-eyed look at the forces arrayed against you might discourage you from anything other than simply doing your job well. But let's apply a small-wins strategy to the problem of getting you promoted.

Choose a small win that satisfies four criteria:

1. If achieved, it will move you closer to your goal.

2. It should be satisfying in itself.

3. It should have leverage in the system.

4. It should be achievable from your present position and with your present resources.

Closer to Your Goal

In keeping with the first criterion, moving closer to your goal, you would not choose volunteering for a committee job in your professional association as a step toward getting a promotion. Although the work might interest you, educate you, and satisfy your social needs, it would probably not help you be promoted (unless your vice president was on the same committee, in which case it might be an excellent choice for a first small win). On the other hand, trying to wangle a separate listing for you and your unit in the company phone book—justified by a need to make it easier for potential trainees to call for information—could be a step in the right direction.

Satisfying in Itself

Next, decide whether the small win you're considering would be satisfying on its own. Would a separate phone listing, headed by your name in brilliant black, be a nice thing to have, even if it didn't lead to a promotion? If your answer is "No way!" then the second criterion says you have not selected a useful small win. After all, your intention is to solve a large problem by cutting it down into achievable segments, not to occupy your time with trivialities. If, however, seeing your name shouting out from the printed page polishes your ego a bit, it will do as a step in your small-wins strategy.

Source of Leverage

Small steps can have large effects if they apply leverage to the system in which your problem is embedded. Will the step you're taking make you or your function better known or generate respect in the eyes of important people? Will it give you access, even tangentially, to the flow of previously unavailable resources? Questions like these help you test whether your small win has enough leverage to make it worthwhile.

How does the enhanced phone book listing measure up? Certainly it will get more attention than did the one-liner "Training Office" that it replaced. More than that, it will signal that your function has significance in the scheme of things, because whoever is in charge of phone listings has seen fit to give you more space. That perception, mistaken or not, might just get you invited to meetings that only your immediate boss, the human resources vice president, had attended. As a result, you gain direct access to information about new projects and other developments. Your phone book ploy may therefore have some leverage potential. That potential would increase dramatically if, because of your attendance at one of those meetings—you will, naturally, have made frequent wise and pertinent comments—a senior vice president who hardly remembered your name before asks for your thoughts about training philosophy for a forthcoming lecture she'll be giving at the local university's business school.

Achievable with Present Resources

If there is no way to carry off your strategy, however brilliant it may be, you are likely to reap more frustration than satisfaction. Your small win must be feasible with the resources of time, influence, and access you have at your fingertips. It may seem a truism, but a prime advantage of a small win is that it is achievable precisely because it is small and unlikely to arouse much resistance.

Usually changing a phone listing doesn't require the approval of senior management because it doesn't consume scarce budget dollars. Other managers are unlikely to raise a fuss for fear of seeming small-minded (even if they are). And you settled on an enlarged phone book listing as your objective because one of your regular golf partners just happens to be the corporate communications manager—the very person who, as one of his less important functions, decides what and who should be listed in the phone directory.

In all its essentials, this small-wins scenario was successfully pulled off by a manager in one of my client organizations. The person in point was promoted to director, later developed into a substantially indispensable person, and then left the company to become an independent consultant. That enterprising training director attributed his successful maneuver principally to the influence of a senior vice president, who, impressed with our hero's grasp of business issues, lobbied to increase the role of the training office.

However, a second circumstance may have been equally important. At one of the meetings to which the manager had formerly not been invited (the human resources vice president was jealous of his prerogatives), he discovered that many of his company's newer projects had substantial training components that, without his knowledge, had been farmed out to local consulting firms. He subsequently bid on them and significantly increased his budget and staff. Much of the power of a small-wins strategy stems from the reality that opening one door—the right one—makes visible other doors that were previously unknown.

Discerning Interconnections and Underlying Causes

Although it's never been scientifically studied, we believe that much of the ability to see into the workings of a problem derives from a capacity to visualize. While the IPs we interviewed all had difficulty verbalizing just what they did in order to see inner relationships, most ventured hesitantly, "I guess I just visualize." To visualize—that is, to form and retain a mental image of some aspect of reality—certainly is unequally distributed among the general run of human beings; it is likely one of those genetically influenced human qualities that unfairly give some of us a 50 percent head start. For example, one of us (Susan) is adept at assembling jigsaw puzzles, while the other (Robert) struggles to keep the shape of a single piece in mind for more than a few seconds.

If you can place yourself in the genetically enhanced group of natural visualizers, take pains to augment that talent by exercising it at every opportunity. It will give you great advantage—probably already has—whether you're an automotive mechanic or an astrophysicist. Fortunately, those of us who were shortchanged by our inheritance can still enhance our ability to discern underlying relationships; after all, we can work with the 50 percent that were more genetically gifted. Whichever group you're in, as the training of combat pilots attests, the capacity to visualize can be developed to some extent by practice. You can supplement it by using questioning and diagramming techniques to surface less obvious aspects of a problem situation. The exercises that follow should help you to develop whatever natural talent has come your way.

Practice Visualizing

Whenever you can, practice visualizing situations. For example, before taking a car trip, study a map of your route and then, closing your eyes, visualize the countryside solely from the car's changes of direction and tilt, engine noises, differences in sounds and echoes as objects are passed, and so forth. Similarly, use whatever knowledge you have to visualize precisely what happens to the fuel in your automobile as it moves through the engine and exhaust system. Try your hand at jigsaw puzzles—especially valuable if you don't enjoy them—concentrating on affixing in your mind areas of the puzzle not yet completed. Visualize either the appearance of the completed picture or—harder— the shapes needed to fill the space.

Create Diagrams

If you can't visualize well, diagram. When faced with a problem, take the time to display the basic facts and relationships that describe the system in which the problem is embedded. Your diagram should show the elements of the problem—that usually means all of the individuals, units, machines, and other entities that are party to the problem—and how they are connected. (You may have to draw a three-dimensional diagram.) Then take these steps:

1. Explicate what happens at each important connection—who does what to whom, who initiates the action, etc.

2. Identify any cross-purposes that show up within each element and in the connections between them. To do this, ask questions like "Who are their customers?"; "What do they each want/need?"; and "Why aren't they getting it?"

3. Identify ways to resolve or mediate the cross-purposes.

These steps are based on the theory—best explicated by W. Edwards Deming—that when systems problems exist, the causes will usually be found at the interconnections of the parts.

One of the IPs in our sample, a corporate troubleshooter, used this approach successfully. He was assigned to diagnose the causes of consistently late deliveries from one factory. The plant manager had tried everything he could think of to fix the problem, but to no avail. As a first step the troubleshooter diagrammed every event from the time a salesperson called on a customer to the time the equipment was delivered, and then identified the potentially weak points in both the communication linkages and the decision-making process. Thus briefed, he visited the offending plant and devoted his time there to digging into the likeliest places for a systems breakdown. Although there were lesser contributing causes, the main source of the problem proved to be the plant manager. That excellent but possibly too conservative administrator insisted on waiting until firm orders were safely in hand before permitting his manufacturing people to gear up for production— a shortsighted stance in a hot and growing market.

Asking Questions That Help Surface Key Elements of the Problem

Our clients pay a great deal of money to be confronted by impertinent and hard-to-answer questions. Luckily for us, such questions needn't be particularly penetrating in order to be useful. In fact, the best are often the most obvious: "What will tell you when you've reached your goal?" or "What are your alternatives?" The value of these and similar questions is that they open the mind to new possibilities.

The following questions are some that we have found most useful for unsettling the minds of our clients:

- What would an ideal solution to this problem look like?

- What individuals and/or units are connected with this problem? Who benefits? Who cares how it is solved? Who is hurt by the problem?

- Over which pieces of the problem do I (we, you) have some control? How much? Could we get more?

- What has worked in the past for problems like this? What hasn't worked, even though we thought it would?

- What are at least three different ways that this problem might be understood?

- From whom might I get a radically different perspective on this problem?

- When did the symptoms of this problem start? When did we first notice something was amiss? What else was happening at that time?

- Is this problem part of a larger disturbance in the scheme of things? (For example, how are other stores in the neighborhood doing?) Do you detect larger system influences on the problem?

Such questions will work for you best when they become part of a routine of inquiry that guides you through any significant issue that comes your way.

Notice that none of the suggested questions start with *why*. "Why" questions elicit plausible—but often incorrect—explanations, even when the answerers are uncertain of just why they believe what they do. Instead of a true, if unsatisfying, "it just feels right," most people will summon up "sensible" reasons, leading you further astray from a deeper understanding of the issue.

A second reason to avoid "why" questions stems from that mental sleight of hand by which explaining a belief to another person converts it into an absolute certainty in the mind of the explainer. It's not completely clear why explaining increases certainty, but there is substantial evidence that it does. Having convinced ourselves (without the benefit of a shred more evidence), we are now much less likely to search for a better explanation—or even recognize it if we should stumble on it.

Finally, "why" questions also tend to provoke defensiveness, an unconscious reaction left over from childhood days, when accusations from grown-ups often took the form of "Why did you tease the cat?" or, "Why didn't you do your homework?" While it's true that digging up plausible answers to those questions exercised our budding imaginations, their intent was obfuscation, not edification.

Since my clients are widely experienced, often brilliant, executives, I've wondered at times why they react to these questions with astonishment, as if I had introduced some novel, never-before-encountered perspective. I have finally concluded that when someone is intently focused on finding an elusive solution to a recalcitrant problem, that person's field of view is excessively narrowed. (It's the same phenomenon that prompts those who capture wild animals for scientific—or commercial—purposes to move in when their prey are fighting or mating.)

Using the Bottom of Your Priority Lists

Pondering which thinking style is most relevant to a task, broadening your perspective, diagramming complex problems, and asking questions all take time. Indispensable people use priority lists to accumulate that time by focusing most of their attention where it belongs: on the bottom of the list, not on the top.

Developing priority lists—that is, setting tasks or objectives in some order of importance—must be the most lauded yet misused planning device in the human repertoire. People misuse these lists by concentrating on the useless end of the list, the top, rather than the helpful end, the bottom. But it is the bottom of the list that will tell you what you are to do poorly or not at all. Then you will have resources left to do whatever is at the top of your list exceptionally well, and you won't get stuck using your evenings and weekends scrambling to finish tasks that should have gotten short shrift anyway.

Studies of successful managers have repeatedly demonstrated that they treat different projects differently, focusing on minutiae in some and dealing cavalierly with others. They work some projects all the way through to completion while letting others bounce along the best way they can. Somewhere along the way, those peak-performing managers learned that, given limited time (an everyday condition in the work world), you cannot do the former unless you also do the latter.

At the very least, a good priority list can keep you from succumbing to that most importuning of phrases, "It's important." Of course it is! Most people with demanding jobs are only asked to do "important" things. But it is inexorably true that when there is not enough time to do all of the important things, some of them will not be done, or they will be done poorly. Usually those left out are the ones currently squeaking less, even though they are often of greater long-term significance. By matching every new task against your priority list, particularly its bottom half, you'll have a better sense of the trade-offs involved when you add something new to a load already full.

Constantly considering priorities will allow you, as a conscientious IP, to steal time from the tasks at the bottom so that you can apply your best thinking skills to those at the top. The next step is to use the cold logic of your priorities to "educate" others to an unyielding fact: If they only focus on what's most important, while ignoring what's least, they will get less value from their (or your) time.

Avoiding Common Errors in Perception and Judgment

It doesn't take too thorough a reading of your local newspaper's business section to remind you that it is not all that unusual for intelligent people to make stupid decisions. This penchant for even the brightest to fall prey to a variety of perceptual and judgmental errors has fascinated students of the human condition for millennia. As you might expect, such unintended foolishness is more likely when motivations and feelings are high and when an established method or formula isn't available, precisely the conditions under which many business decisions are made. Even indispensable people fall into these traps occasionally; they just do it less.

Devoting Equal Time to All Decisions

Decision theorists have suggested that many decisions are of little consequence, so people should make them quickly, based solely on the information at hand. The reason for being so cavalier with those decisions is, of course, to allow enough time and energy for thoroughly considering the few that have serious consequences or that will only be well implemented if they are understood and accepted. The problem is that most people tend to devote equal time to every one of their decisions. They ruminate too long over matters that should be either quickly decided or delegated, and decisions that deserve far more careful thought get squeezed into the time that is left.

Deciding Too Soon

There are times when quickly evolving life situations call for fast action without much thought—to put out a sudden kitchen fire, for example. During such times, we fall back on unconscious action habits that we hope will be adequate for the emergency. But acting on impulse tends to interfere with bringing full intellectual resources to bear on a problem. While endlessly analyzing is no better, grasping the first solution that comes to mind, even when it has some underlying merit, often leaves significant parts of the problem unresolved. This approach starts a cycle of fix it, then fix it again—a recurring tendency of overly enthusiastic Realist thinkers.

The "What Assumptions?" Error

Most decisions are based on some assumptions. People make the "what assumptions?" error when they forget to check whether their assumptions are valid. For example, it might be reasonable to conclude that if sales increase, you will need to hire more staff. If you start hiring without waiting for solid indications of an upturn in business, you have committed the "what assumptions?" error.

The Sunk Cost Error

From a strictly economic standpoint, you should ignore the amount of prior investment when deciding on a future investment in the same project. However, that bit of wisdom is often lost in the push and pull of life. People make the sunk cost error; they try to correct an unwise investment by investing even more. Anyone who has ever remodeled a house has learned this awful truth: the greater the investment in time and money that follows from a decision, the less likely that decision will be critically examined while it is being implemented. Here are some causes:

- You fool yourself into believing that more improvements can make a failing project succeed.

- You increase your investment to maintain your self-esteem or the esteem of others. ("If I let this thing fold after two years and $2 million, they'll never trust my judgment again. I've got to make it work.")

- You mentally place the reference point for additional investment at the current investment level. Therefore, added increments don't seem all that significant when viewed against the loss of what has already been invested. ("We're only talking about forty grand more to finally get something out of the half million we've already put into this thing.")

The Assuming-Similarities Error

Most people assume that others generally see the world pretty much as they do. If you make this error, you may be surprised or even shocked when those with different thinking styles, motivations, or backgrounds don't buy your carefully prepared proposal.

The Proving-You're-Right Error

The proving-you're-right error involves using information to confirm a previously held theory or belief. It has two variations:

In the first variation, you neglect to collect information other than that which will prove or disprove your theory. For example, you believe the lighting level in your store affects sales, so you test your theory by changing the light configuration in one of your showrooms. Sure enough, the sales level of that room increases, and your confidence in your theory soars. Unfortunately, your high spirits may be ill founded, because you neglected to measure the other factors that might affect sales, such as temperature difference, the reaction of sales staff to *any* change in the showroom (commonly called the Hawthorne effect), and so forth.

You also commit this error if you ignore, or discount, data that don't confirm your belief. For example, you believe that all accountants are rule-bound "bean counters," and you see plenty of those. If you encounter accountants who are imaginative problem solvers, you explain them away as special cases, somehow "different," and your strongly held belief stays intact.

Forgetting the Regression to the Mean

A more subtle trap is forgetting a statistics principle called regression to the mean. When repeated measures are taken of a characteristic of any group, the measurements will gradually come closer to the average of that characteristic. This is especially noticeable when the initial measures are either very high or very low. If you don't remember the regression to the mean, you might think that the change from these early measures to the average are really showing a change in what you are measuring.

To see how this works, imagine that you set up a new customer complaint procedure, and you tested it with periodic surveys. Initially the ratings of the service were poor, but after a few months you are pleased to find they have gradually improved. Content with those positive findings, you discontinue the surveys in the belief that they showed your new procedure brought about an improvement in customer attitudes. In fact, attitudes never changed. The improved ratings were simply an artifact of the tendency of repeated measures in any sample to regress to the mean.

Misreading Averages

Often people misunderstand statements such as "The teenagers have an average height of five feet." Many people think this means that most of the teenagers measured are five feet tall. In reality, of the six who were measured, four could have been four feet tall, and the other two could have been seven-foot basketball players. If you had ordered a supply of clothing for six five-footers, you'd be out of luck.

Losing Sight of the Denominator

The media frequently report fractional improvement in the cure rate of some awful disease. What they leave out (because it might detract from the news value of the report) is that the previous incidence rate of the illness was only 5 in 10,000. Now only 3.75 of 10,000 will fall ill with that disease, which only infects 5,000 people a year anyway. While the numerator—what's happened—is of interest, unless you know the full context—the denominator—you should be leery of drawing conclusions.

The Faith-in-Small-Samples Error

Have you ever tested a plan on a small sample? Say, you asked five people in your office, your neighbor, and your brother-in-law, and they all agreed that your plan was right on. If you implement it on that basis, you have committed the faith-in-small-samples error. Does that bring the "New Coke/Classic Coke" debacle to mind?

Now that you've read through this compendium of all-too-human tendencies to err, cycle back and mark the ten or so that you think may at times slip into your own problem-solving process. While it is useful to spot these errors wherever they show up, most of us tend to favor some over others. Think of them as camouflaged pitfalls, easy to avoid when you know they are there.

Additional Aids to Increasing Your Thinking Power

Don't limit yourself to the ideas in this book. You can further expand your ability to think like an indispensable person by using the ideas of mentors and other books.

Learning from Mentors

You can learn a lot about problem solving from indispensables if you can induce them to mentor you. You might know IPs in your organization or in business or professional organizations; they may even be among your friends. Keep in mind that their willingness to help you may depend on their perception that you are "worthy" of help. Tell them of your other efforts at self-improvement and your intention to go it alone if they feel unable to help you.

If they agree, you'll gain the most by sitting with them while they work on a problem. Ask them to think out loud so you can see how they approach problems, and probe with questions such as "What thoughts preceded that guess [or conclusion]?" Avoid asking for an explanation of how they solve problems. An intellectual discourse on how problems should be solved will be of little enlightenment, and maybe even misleading, because it may bear little resemblance to what actually is going on in their heads.

Learning from Books

Some people can learn to polish their skills from books; others need more hands-on instruction. If you are one of the former, you may want to read the many recent references that elaborate on how to think penetratingly. Some offer practical exercises that have proved to be useful. The following books are listed in the References.

Mindfulness, by Ellen J. Langer, describes the ways in which even the brightest of us can proceed through much of our work and family lives in a mindless fashion. Langer then tells how to become more mindful, thereby accomplishing more and feeling better about yourself.

The Art of Thinking by Allen F. Harrison and Robert Bramson, provides further elaboration on styles of thinking.

Intelligence Applied, by Robert J. Sternberg, is subtitled *Understanding and Increasing Your Intellectual Skills*, and that is what it is about. Sternberg has extensively studied how people think and is a leader in the development of new theories of intelligence. This book has exercises for assessing and developing various cognitive skills, including what he calls "practical intelligence."

Thought and Knowledge: An Introduction to Critical Thinking and an accompanying workbook, *Thinking Critically About Critical Thinking*, both by Diane F. Halpern, are college texts, which makes them particularly useful because Halpern is careful to fully explain everything. While the exercises deal with everyday life outside of the work setting, the skills apply anywhere.

7

Enhancing Your IP Interpersonal Skills

It is true that indispensable people, as a group, relate well in certain specific ways. But it's equally true that they are not identical peas in the personality pod. They differ as much as any randomly selected collection of people in being friendly, charming, charismatic, warmly sympathetic, and leader-like. Consider, for example, two indispensable people as seen by the same corporate executive:

> Tony Furillo is now a vice president and general manager, but I first knew him when he was in production. The thing about Tony is that you could always count on him to see a job through, difficult or not. He still has lots of

drive and energy, and a real feel for solving technical problems, but he's also great with people, no matter who they are. For example, I've seen him hold a meeting on the factory floor, turning forty demoralized blue-collars around so they're charged up and inspired and feeling valuable.

Yeah, I guess he's what you might call a charismatic person, very articulate, well liked by everyone—but he's also a very straight shooter. He lets people know when they've done a good job, but he dusts them off plenty when they haven't. Either way, they seem to keep on liking him. I think, in part, it's because he has clarity about what needs to be done, and he keeps everyone's eyes on that. People trust him.

Then there's Winn, who in many ways is absolutely the opposite of Tony. He's quiet, not very outgoing, pretty serious most of the time, not even what you'd call very friendly. But at the same time he's—I don't know—accessible I guess is the best word. A lot of people at every level use him for advice, me included. He's head of MIS, so he has access to a lot of what's going on, but more than that, he has a deep understanding of the business— every part of it. He can see the important issues and anticipate what needs to be done. One thing you always know is that he won't bullshit you or make a big deal out of nothing.

You know, what I said at first about Winn might have made him sound like a cold fish, but actually, in a lot of ways he's very sympathetic, especially if you're having problems. He's a good listener. At least, he listens a lot, and then when he says something, you really take it seriously.

Certainly, Tony and Winn were not cast out of the same mold, yet each has acquired certain relationship skills well enough to stand out as an unusually valuable employee. In this chapter you'll find suggestions for developing those interpersonal skills: engendering trust, communicating candidly without provoking defensiveness, effectively helping others, relating well regardless of status differences, and mediating disagreements. And in case you already have a reputation for less-than-adequate skills in any of these areas, we conclude with a section on identifying and changing a negative image.

As you peruse the balance of this chapter, keep in mind that the best way to grow in these areas is to set graduated tasks for yourself that are neither too easy nor too hard. If they're easy, they'll bore you and not add much to your feeling of mastery. If they are too demanding or uncomfortable, you may find yourself letting the whole thing drop. The trick is to select a series of activities that push you just beyond your comfort level but not so far that you feel overwhelmed. Remember that concentrating on what you're learning will get you further than a sole focus on how well you're doing. Save that for six months down the line. The evidence strongly suggests that you'll build confidence faster and will at length achieve more when you look less at progress toward some outside goal—the sales you've made—and more at how you go about what you do and what you're learning from it. It's just another example of the value of keeping your eyes on the process rather than on the goal.

Engendering Trust and Confidence

Although they were not at all alike in many ways, Tony and Winn both had the trust and confidence of their associates. They were trusted because they listened and because their motives were never suspect, and they earned confidence because they promised only what they could produce. If any IP attribute can be considered prime, it is a knack for engendering trust and confidence, a fusion of basic honesty with a can-do attitude and an assiduous dedication to three basic rules for maintaining solid relations with others:

1. Listen first.

2. Don't tell, ask.

3. Be up-front without being one up.

Honesty in a Relativistic World

Even if we believe that honesty of purpose, word, and deed is, or should be, everyone's goal, we live in a world that takes a considerably more relaxed view. Most of us constantly confront pressures—sometimes compelling, sometimes subtly seductive—to be less than fully honest. Among the less than honest practices we've seen during our years of consulting are outright falsification of data to give the appearance of success, to hide mistakes, or to evade responsibility; tax evasion (petty and otherwise); embezzlements (from artfully inflating expense accounts to cooking the books shown to government auditors); bribes, taken and offered (from cushy employment opportunities after retirement to vendor and customer kickbacks). All these are at times done under that sort of corporate aegis in which one hand carefully avoids looking at what the other hand is doing. This brief list is only intended to suggest the range of unethical practices, from slightly dishonest to the downright immoral, in which you may be—or perhaps, have been—tempted, inveigled, invited, or even commanded to engage.

The point of naming this behavior is not to decry the present state of public morality or prescribe a code of behavior, for we each must come to terms with our own ethical self. Rather, you should remember that in today's world, maintaining high ethical standards is not always easy, even when your intentions are thoroughly upright. While the ubiquity of this state of affairs is discouraging, a consistent theme throughout our interviews was that IPs behave according to high personal standards. Certainly that has been true of those with whom we have been intimately acquainted. The behavior of IPs demonstrates that it is possible to stay your own person in the midst of assorted pressures and temptations to bend the truth.

You'll better your chances of not being swept off a principled path by staying alert to the more insidious temptations to double-deal. Here are a few of them that might erode anyone's best intentions to stay straightforward.

"Only Good News Allowed"

Whether they are the heads of small businesses or hierarchical executives, people in charge deeply and sometimes desperately want to hear only about wins, never about losses. Not only are these people professionally committed to the success of their organizations, but their personal success and—perhaps more important—their self-esteem may seem to depend upon a constant stream of good news. At best, this guarantees a watering down of information, abetted by both the sender and the receiver. "We might not make our quota this month," is the sender's version of "we won't," but a hopeful boss translates it as, "There's a slight chance that we will."

"Only the Numbers Count"

When managers expect consistently increasing profits, they distort processes like Management by Objectives, which was initially developed as a way of allowing employees to participate in goal setting. As one client put it, "Around here, no matter what they say to your face, if you don't make your numbers, no one cares whether you've done your job right or not." In such an environment, the temptation to inflate (or make up) those numbers can be constant and pressing.

"Up the Organization, Whatever It Takes"

Here are some beliefs—partly true, partly untrue, and usually untested—that creep into many corporate cultures:

- Our survival as an organization is more important than the needs of our employees, clients, customers, or the public.

- The only real objective of a profit-making organization is increasing profit. Everything else must serve this goal.

- What's good for the organization is good for whoever is associated with it.

Certainly not all, or even most, organizational leaders subscribe to these statements without qualification, though we have met some for whom they constituted a kind of business catechism. In fact, studies of the most effective executives have repeatedly shown that most of them see profits as the hoped-for result of good service, high quality, operational efficiency, and the development of useful products. However, sometimes the decisions made at the top make it hard to believe that these are really the bottom-line values that drive the organization.

When increasing profits seem the only genuine goal, placing ethical or social needs first can seem like heresy, and we all know what closed societies do about heretics. Thus, organizational settings induce some people to do things they would not have considered doing in their personal lives.

"Everybody's Doing It"

In a world in which the news media put entertainment value above accuracy, where publishers' secret payments place books on the "bestseller" list, isn't bending the rules OK when "everybody's doing it"? Shady ethics in the workplace are nothing new, and given the pressures we've already touched upon, it's unlikely that the situation will improve much in the future. The knowledge that others are behaving immorally without censure, and often with considerably enriched purses, can undermine your own resolution to behave ethically.

Why Be Ethical?

As you might expect, the first step toward behaving as you think you ought is by far the most sizable one: deciding that you want to. If everyone is fudging a bit or looking the other way, if it's as much trouble as it sometimes seems, what could possibly make it worthwhile to walk the straight and narrow? Of the many reasons for making a commitment to stay honest and upright, three seem particularly relevant to this book: to avoid salving your conscience by punishing yourself, to provide a bulwark against the self-sabotaging tricks your own mind can play, and to gain others' trust by being trustworthy.

You Might Fool Yourself, but Not Your Conscience

In his most important book, *Man for Himself*, psychologist and social philosopher Erich Fromm suggests that those who deviate from their own deeply held personal standards will in some fashion make themselves pay for it. Our own experience in observing the lives of others, as well as living with ourselves and those closest to us, has convinced us that Fromm's assertion is fundamentally true. You might find several ways to punish yourself for slips and slides:

• *Getting yourself in trouble*—The media are full of tales of very smart people with very clever schemes who then stupidly get themselves caught and publicly punished.

• *Getting sick*—Recent findings about how the mind and emotions affect the immune system reveal that your conscience can indeed kill you, thereby interfering with your plans to become indispensable.

• *Making yourself miserable*—If any of the aforementioned seem too extreme, that part of you that judges everything you do stands ready to treat you to those old standbys: tension, depression, sleeplessness, rampant indigestion, and other assorted tricks for interfering with your enjoyment of work or anything else.

Your Mind, a Subtle Saboteur

If we only needed to decide between deliberate lying and staying the ethical course, our moral lives would be much simpler. But our good intentions may not be enough when they conflict with nature's dictum to go after what we want. For example, it's been well substantiated that our desires, fears, and wishes will strongly affect how we remember and interpret past events. That crafty, unconscious part of us whose only mandate is to look out for number one can twist a decision to act ethically into something quite different.

Take the case of Bert Ramsey, the managing partner of a financial advisement firm. Eighteen months before, in my presence, he had promised his partners that if gross income failed to reach a certain specified level within two years, he would relinquish leadership of the firm. Now, a year and a half later, it was apparent that his plans for developing the business were taking longer to bear fruit than he'd expected, so I suggested that he should try to renegotiate his promise. "No need," he cheerfully informed me, "I have two and a half more years to go before I'm up for review."

I'm certain that he was not trying to mislead me. He was sure his recollection was as clear as could be: he had given himself four years to meet his goals, not two.

Is it fudging the issue to say that Bert was not dishonest, that his memory just deceived him? Probably not. The results of many studies demonstrate the mutability of human memory. What was even more compelling to us were instances of our own "innocent" —meaning that we were unaware of any shady intent— but self-serving recollections.

Another way our mind can sabotage our best efforts at honesty is with a way of thinking that makes ethical questions seem irrelevant. Some people, because of their thinking style, are seldom troubled by ethical questions. For example, those Realist thinkers we touched upon in the last chapter tend to lose patience with anything that cannot be directly sensed, especially such ethereal concepts as ethical notions and others' feelings. They are not about to let such seemingly irrelevant matters stand in the way of capturing a prize. Realist thinkers do at times suffer pangs of conscience, but the point at which they begin to be troubled may be much further over the line than others believe is appropriate.

In their own ways, other thinking styles pose different ethical challenges. Speculating Synthesist thinkers can confuse what might be so with what is. Pragmatists may compromise their principles for an immediate payoff or to avoid "unnecessary" hassles. Concrete-thinking Analysts may put a clean balance sheet above "softheaded" social needs. Even true-blue Idealists are often less than candid in an effort to avoid distressing someone.

To Be Trusted, You Have to Be Trustworthy

Most of us don't do a very convincing job when we try to be devious. True, our coworkers don't often challenge our attempts, but that's because the signals we send—

more nonverbal than verbal—don't shout, "I'm bending the truth!" or, "Hey, chump, I'm taking advantage of you!"; they simply make others edgy. If you are less than trustworthy, edgy coworkers may stay pleasant because there's nothing they can quite put their fingers on. Still, some will simply avoid you because you worry them, and they are unlikely to trust or confide in you. Edgy bosses are more inclined to micromanage you and at the earliest opportunity trade you in for someone who doesn't make them so nervous. That may considerably dimminish your prospects for becoming indispensable.

Not to be too negative about it, however, there is a convenient way to lie with gusto and still escape detection: tell others, especially your bosses, only what they want to hear. You can be sure that the recipients of your verbal largesse will cooperate with any optimistic obfuscations, no matter how bizarre, and will often pitch in with creative rationalizations when things don't quite pan out. While this ploy will not help you become an IP of the sort we've earlier described, your organization might well keep you on for years as a kind of pet, at least until a less gullible boss comes along.

How to Build Trust in the Real World

It's easy to conclude that every one of us has some dishonest leanings, even if we don't consider ourselves untrustworthy. As children, most of us learned to be less than candid in order to avoid punishment or embarrassment, to keep friendships, to obtain rewards that we might not otherwise have enjoyed. Often our dishonesty worked. Does that mean that we're all stuck with these tendencies to err? Well, yes and no. They do flow naturally from our experiences and the way our minds work, but they are not imperatives. The more we can recognize when we get an impulse to compromise with the truth, and the clearer we are that we *intend* to stay on the honest side, the easier it is to stick with what we believe we ought to do. If you are familiar with the foregoing litany of ethical pitfalls, you can do what indispensable people do: sidestep them and allow your own personal standards to guide you through the maze.

Compared to their less honest counterparts, IPs are not essentially different. They simply tend to be dishonest less often where it doesn't count much and, when necessary, do what they can to set the record straight. To be more like an IP, you need to acknowledge your own favorite kinds of dishonesty. Do you withhold information so you'll look good? Do you exaggerate or minimize to enhance your reputation? Do you soft-pedal your judgments to avoid distressing others? The ways are endless. The best you can do is to stay alert for signs that you're slipping, and stop yourself in time. Thus, when you feel sympathetic pangs and hear yourself begin to edge into "I guess it's OK," you'll correct yourself to ". . . but I can't really buy into your plan; here's why."

An Almost Sure Test

An almost sure test of whether you may be stepping over a moral boundary is your ability—or, rather, your inability—to discuss what you're contemplating with someone whose respect you care about: a spouse, child, parent, or close friend. If you'd rather not tell them, your reluctance signals that if you do, you will make yourself pay for it.

Take Steps to Be Honest When It's Relevant and Important

When the ethical issues are not clear-cut, how to respond may not be obvious. Some years ago, a wise mentor suggested a rule of thumb that has been helpful in such situations. The rule is simple: If the matter is both relevant to your purposes and important by your own standard, be candid even if you don't really want to. Otherwise, you can play it as it lies (pun intended). For example, if your coworker suggested splitting a dinner check even though you knew your portion cost more than his, you might go along because, while relevant to what you were doing, it didn't seem very consequential. Similarly, you might ignore your suspicion that an acquaintance was embezzling from his own company, even though the amounts involved were sizable, on the basis that the misbehavior, while important, was not relevant to your work or life. Honesty becomes something that is based on its relevance to you.

The mentor (and friend) who gave me this advice was Walcott Beatty, Emeritus Professor of Psychology at San Francisco State University. He pointed out to me that honesty in communication often discomfits those who give it and distresses those for whom it is intended; thus, said Professor Beatty, honesty ought to be used sparingly and with discrimination.

When Pressured by an Ethical Dilemma, Point Out Your Discomfort

At times—we hope they are few and far between—you may be faced with a proposal to do something that violates your own notion of what is ethical or proper. Whether it's an order to downplay a product's unsafe feature, instructions to unfairly fire an employee to save a superior's reputation, or an unspoken assumption that you'll look the other way when a coworker stocks his home workshop at your employer's expense, you may feel compelled to go along with something that is more or less repugnant to you. The dilemma can be agonizingly real. Do you accede and suffer the erosion of your self-respect, not to mention the self-punishing hits from your conscience, or refuse and face the loss of position or the disapprobation of your colleagues?

The best way out of that dilemma is a response that has more power than one would expect from so simple a phrase. The phrase is "I'm really uncomfortable with that." It can help you to stay forthright, yet it does not impugn anyone else's morality or good judgment. You do open yourself to a rejoinder like "I guess that's your problem," which indeed it is. However, you can acknowledge as much and then describe just why you are uncomfortable, always presenting the issue as your problem, not implying that it ought to be anyone else's. You might suggest alternatives to the proposed action, not in the least implying that others are evil, stupid, or uncaring. There is much power in this dance. We have seen rambunctious top executives who were pursuing ill-advised courses of action become suddenly nonplussed because someone has pointed out how that particular emperor was unclothed. What they had previously ignored or prettily disguised was now fully exposed.

Even when the action you're trying to resist is not heinous but simply—at least in your eyes—not the best way to go, consider sticking with a quiet, non-confronting statement about your continuing discomfort. Such a statement is often far more effective than well-organized arguments against particular points, since every argument will surely draw a spate of counterarguments. Instead, if you quietly refuse to deny your discomfort, you should prevail. As a bonus, you will also have earned a reputation as someone who is not only courageous, but wise.

Communicating Candidly Without Provoking Defensiveness

Anyone with nerve can candidly put forth facts, opinions, and conclusions, but as an indispensable person, you'll need to develop skill at presenting your views in a nonchallenging, nonattacking manner. Here are some suggestions for engaging others with your openness rather than intimidating them, provoking defensiveness, and leaving them feeling one down.

Listen First

Rule Number One, applicable in any interpersonal situation, is, *Always* listen first. Don't decide what you think—in fact, don't think about what you think—until you've heard what there is to hear. By heading you off from those perception and judgment errors recounted in Chapter 6, Rule Number One will save you wasted time and effort. Most people will accept a decision—even one they disagree with—when they feel the decision maker heard their point of view.

If you see yourself as a Pragmatist, Analyst, or Realist thinker, take this rule to heart. Even though you might have to stretch to practice it, it can save some embarrassing moments.

While attending an executive off-site meeting, one of my clients—let's call him Ralph—was provoked into action by an urgent phone call from his wife, who was concerned because their fifteen-year-old son and a pal had driven off in the family car. As he was striding to the door, I reminded him of Rule Number One. Then he was out the door—to calm his wife, I supposed, and to see that his son was properly dealt with.

An hour later, Ralph returned to tell this story: "When I got home, the car was nowhere in sight, and my wife had left for work. I found Charlie in his bedroom, getting something out of a drawer. I grabbed his shoulder, jerked him around, and was ready to go full blast when I remembered Rule Number One. It turns out that he had simply moved the car back behind the garage so that he and his pal could practice some plays—they're both on the football team. My wife had looked out the window just at the wrong moment, couldn't see Charlie, couldn't see the car, and panicked. What Charlie did may not have been entirely right, but on the other hand, I've let him practice starts and stops on our driveway. Anyway, I will live by Rule Number One from now on."

Although it does not directly apply to this discussion, Rule Number Three is, Never give full credence to the first description of an incident. Rule Number Two, of course, is, Never forget Rule Number One.

Ask If Others Want Honesty

It's easier to be calmly candid with others when they have indicated that honesty is what they want. We often use this approach in our consultations: "I've seen something that might be a problem; do you want to hear about it?" It's especially effective when you need to be straightforward with someone in authority or in a power position—a boss or a customer, for example.

Even better is to set the stage for open communication early on by asking, "If I see something you're doing that might be improved (or that isn't in line with your best interests), do you want me to mention it?" Yes, you have seemingly created a social situation in which it is difficult for anyone to say no without appearing ungracious, to say the least. Yet the real pressure on the other person comes not from any sort of social blackmail, but from the logic of the situation itself: It is irrational to refuse information on possible improvements. (It's the same logic that moves IPS to seek wide input before deciding.)

When others have asked you to be forthright, they will do their best to listen to what you have to say; as a bonus, they will be less likely to react defensively. That may be the reason why some people respond to this ploy with a smile, clearly understanding that they have been set up and even admiring how neatly it was done. Under those circumstances, a possibly tense situation is converted into a conversation about possible problems and potential solutions.

Avoid Accusation-Defense-Reaccusation

There is a communication pattern so entertaining to witness that it's been given a name, accusation-defense-reaccusation. It starts anytime Person A feels accused by a statement or a question that Person B may or may not have intended as an accusation: "Are you up on what our customers want these days, John?" Feeling accused, John will typically respond with some sort of a defense: "I talk to my customers every day, Jane," quickly followed by a reaccusation hurled at Jane: "And where are those customer service guidelines you were supposed to send out?" Whether Jane's original question was indeed meant to accuse or was a simple query, Jane will defend her honor with a neat retort, zapping out a reaccusation of her own, and so on.

Those who have studied this mutually frustrating pattern have long pointed out its most insidious feature: While it sounds to both parties as if they are having a problem-solving discussion, in reality, the more they go at it, the further they are from finding a solution to anything. Of course, if Person B is intimidating enough, she may hear only the defense; person A will hold his reaccusation in reserve for use as an "I gotcha" attack when Person B slips up, as we all must do.

Accusations seldom elicit an acknowledgment of problem behavior. Like nagging and scolding, they are more likely to prompt a defensive determination to maintain the very behavior they were supposed to correct.

Instead of Accusing, Report Your Perception or Reaction

How do we tell others that their behavior needs correcting without starting a stultifying chain reaction? One effective approach is to report, as matter-of-factly as possible, what you've seen, heard, or inferred, implying that any of these perceptions is subject to error. You are not holding yourself superior to the people you're addressing; you are merely calling it as you see it. The general tone to try for is something like this: "This is what I've noticed . . . ," followed by as clear a description as you can give of whatever it is that needs attention. In the earlier example, Jane might have said, "I've noticed that you seldom review the monthly marketing research reports, and that's got me thinking, 'Is John so focused on selling that he's missing out on useful information?' "

Don't be put off if you still pick up a kind of hedging defense: "Do those guys at headquarters really know what's going on?" John is no fool, and he's been around long enough to know that many simple-sounding questions *are* accusations in disguise. Just stay with simply reporting what you've noticed, and you should eventually hear, "Do you really think there's something that I ought to look at in those reports?"—the start of a potentially useful conversation. (Although our topic is how to be direct without provoking defensiveness, some situations call for being painfully direct. Recall that many IPs believe that their start on the path to indispensability began with a severe reprimand from someone they respected.)

Don't Be Thrown Off by Denial and Blame

From time to time, you may need to be critical of some aspect of a coworker's behavior. You can save yourself from some fruitless chafing by keeping in mind that criticism almost invariably begets denial and blame in that order. The first response is often to deny that anything untoward occurred at all ("I didn't do that," or a more indirect "I don't usually do it that way"). If the denial doesn't send you on your way, there's always a second line of defense: shifting the responsibility to something or someone else ("FedEx doesn't pick up on Saturday," or "The policy's not very clear"). If neither of those ploys succeeds in deflecting blame, the employee may try blaming *you*, the bringer of bad news ("If you had told me before, I wouldn't still have these problems").

To counter your exasperation at these responses, remind yourself that denial and blame are the first steps in anyone's change process. If you wait it out and continue to confront them with their behavior and the effects it's having, you can often move them to stage three in the change process: acknowledging that they are doing what they do and that they may in fact be part of a problem.

Avoid One-Up, One-Down Interactions

No one likes feeling one down, whether pushed there by a surly teammate or by the upraised middle finger of a driver who has just cut you off. To be fair to that arrogant driver (or that equally obnoxious teammate), there is much satisfaction in relegating another human being to that inferior position that we call one down, thereby elevating yourself to the exalted state of being one up. But this satisfaction comes at a price. Those who feel one down seldom try to move back to an equal position with the person they believe has demeaned them. Instead, they do everything they can to become one up, restarting the whole process in the opposite direction.

The communication techniques we've thus far touched on in this chapter all minimize the possibility that others will feel one down. There are also several additional methods that cost little but will enable the recipient of critical feedback to save face.

Depersonalize Criticism

"You are inferior to me," is the message that makes feeling one down so hurtful. It's worthwhile to do what you can to minimize that implication. One way is to frame any judgmental comments as having been forced on you by your organizational role. You are not trying to evade responsibility for your opinions, just to get across that you are not arrogantly assuming a holier-than-thou position. If you are a manager, you might say, "I know that you'd rather not hear this, but my job calls for me to evaluate how you're doing and tell you what I see." To a coworker you might say, "For the good of the team, I need to tell you that I've noticed . . ."

Will that eliminate the sting of having been judged and found somehow wanting? Likely not, but that wasn't what you were after anyway. Your objective was to dispel, at least in part, any implication that you think of yourself as a superior human being telling an inferior human being how he should do his job.

Convey Respect to Soften Criticism

The more that those you spend time with believe you understand and respect them, the less attacked they will feel when you point out their shortcomings. Therefore, it's worthwhile to briefly acknowledge their good intentions or particular competencies when treating them to any negatively tinged judgments: "I realize you're just trying to help, but . . . ," or, "Your facility with Spanish has certainly been helpful around here, but when you chat up the customers in Spanish, I'm not sure how to proceed with the sales call."

Assume Ignorance of Off-Putting Behaviors

Despite two decades of helping individual clients learn about, acknowledge, and manage difficult aspects of their behavior, we continue to be surprised at how obtuse people can be about how, and how much, they annoy and otherwise put off those with whom they live and work. For that reason, no matter how glaring you believe another's behavioral flaws to be, that person may not realize their impact. Therefore, when you try to point out the effects of those flaws, you will get a better response if you precede your comments with a statement like these: "My guess is you're not really aware that you . . . ," or, "I know I've always joked about it, so I can see why you haven't known how much your phone conversations distract me."

Advise by Asking Rather Than Telling

As any parent of teenagers has discovered, advice, even when asked for, often provokes resistance rather than enlightenment. Much less of this disconcerting phenomenon occurs when we pose our suggestions as questions.

If a client, excited about a well-funded television advertising campaign, waxes enthusiastic about beefing up the sales force, I force myself to resist advising against making such a move too soon, even though I know that anticipated sales often don't pan out. I have had more success with "Would there be a point in waiting until the first results of the campaign are in before staffing up?" than with "Why don't you wait . . ." The former will usually prompt a thoughtful consideration, whereas the latter often elicits an obsessively lengthy explanation of why waiting would be a poor idea.

The utility of question over comment is that telling conveys an underlying message that I have a superior grasp of the situation, thereby nudging my client slightly one down. Asking, in contrast, respects the other person's experience and intelligence.

The value of questioning over advising confirms itself to me when (only occasionally, I hope) I slip into a telling mode and am reminded by the listener's stiffening posture that I've pushed when I should have pulled.

Effectively Helping Others

Succinctly put, IPs are helpful but not too helpful. They are willing, even generous, supporters of their coworkers when they judge that their help is really needed, but not much interested in assisting any they deem capable of managing on their own. While IPs seem comfortable with the mantle of "mentor," they are never described as know-it-alls, or superior in attitude. The following suggestions will help you to stay within those limits.

One Down Revisited

It is disheartening when well-meant offers of help are coldly received. It's easy to forget that even though—perhaps especially when—help is needed, being helped can leave the recipient feeling inferior and one down in the relationship. True, people who are efficacious know that asking for help does not connote inferiority, merely that they have not yet acquired everything possible in the way of skill and knowledge. But if you are going to offer help, consider taking some useful steps to minimize the resistance that masks an understandable wish not to feel one down:

- *Take a one-down position yourself*—By openly admitting to one or another of your human imperfections, you pull the figurative rug out from under any such thoughts in others. For example, you might lead into a suggestion with "I've had trouble myself keeping all the product names straight, but when I organize them this way . . ." Psychologists point out that people interpret taking a one-down position as a sign of strength.

- *Ask what the other person has tried*—Before providing ideas or suggestions, first ask, "What have you tried?" or "What has worked best for you?" Such questions allow others to show their competence and grasp of the situation, establishing that you are equals rather than that they are novices seeking wisdom from a superior.

You'll gain twice from these techniques. First, you'll lessen the chance that those you are helping will feel that they *are* less than you, rather than simply *knowing* less than you. Therefore, you will increase the likelihood that in the future they will act independently, so you will probably not hear repeated knocks on your door for more and more help. Second, those you help will be more likely to attend to the matter at hand, rather than worrying about who is one up or one down, so they'll learn faster and need you less.

Provide Alternatives, Not Advice

Instead of dishing out advice and suggestions, summarize the alternatives available to the person you're helping, the probable consequences of taking each alternative, and a problem-solving approach that might lead your coworker to find the useful solution. For example, here are some ideas for someone who needs to conduct marketing research: "It looks to me as if your choices are a customer survey, convening some focus groups, or simply hanging around store counters, listening to what customers say. I gather that a survey might be more than your budget can stand. If so, wouldn't your best bet be to think about the kind of results you might get from the other two methods? Then select the one that will enable you to improve customer service right away."

Help Others Switch Perspectives

Psychologist Ellen Langer has suggested that the greatest help you can give someone who's trying to make a difficult decision is to help him become "uncommitted" to his favorite way of approaching a problem. For example, these comments suggest a new way to approach a hiring decision: "Look, Sam, I know you like to be very scientific about every new hire, but what would you learn if you just intuitively rank the three top candidates? I'll do the same, and we'll see how much we agree."

You might also consider passing on a few of the Chapter 6 suggestions for broadening perspective.

Provide the Kind of Help That's Needed

People ask for help for a variety of reasons: for information, for a ready-made solution they think you might have, to break loose their own creativity, or even to rid themselves of an emotional load that is washing out any chance they can think sensibly at all. Addressing the wrong need, no matter how effectively, will equally frustrate both parties, so take the time to identify what they're really after.

Ask yourself, "What does this particular person need at this particular time?" Is it an appeal for a confidence boost disguised as a request for information, or is a dependent person at your door because it's easier to ask than to look up the answer? If it's the former, ask how she'll use the information, so she'll see that she really knows a lot already. If it's the latter, walk that lazy person over to the appropriate information source and stand by while he does what he should have done in the first place.

In any case, be especially alert for signs of emotional overload. Even though someone may seem to be searching for substantive help, he won't benefit from any that you offer until the internal pressure has been somewhat alleviated. Wounded people have all sorts of complicated things going on inside them, none of which are your responsibility. But a sympathetic ear or a bit of companionship can often alleviate tension, anxiety, or self-doubt enough to enable them to tackle whatever problems brought them to you in the first place. So, instead of pushing information or trying to coax them into feeling better, listen for a while, try a little perspective humor, or even offer your company at lunch or after work.

Watch for Codependency

If you find that you are constantly providing help to the same others, check to make sure that you haven't slipped into a codependent role. Most of us are aware of the characteristics of dependency: an unwillingness to accept responsibility, the assumption that one ought to be cared for by others, and a willingness to engage in almost any sort of finagling to ensure that the care will be given. In a codependent role, you become a dependent coworker's partner in crime, taking on the responsibility for seeing that a presumably adult person is saved from the consequences of his own behavior. Codependent people often report an insistent inner voice that says, "A really good person always offers help when asked." It *is* often difficult to distinguish requests for assistance that are justified from an impassioned appeal by one who would prefer that you do work that is rightfully his. After all, isn't it a part of an owner's perspective that "We're all responsible to see that the package goes out the door"?

One fairly reliable test that you've become a patsy is how frequently people ask you to help with the same sort of problem. Do you repeatedly bail out the same individual so that report deadlines are met? An even better test is your growing feeling of resentment as you continue to dutifully give up your weekend to finish the report. If you make a habit of picking up the slack, others—especially dependent others—will let you, and you'll find it "necessary" more and more often. In that sad scenario, everyone loses: you because you're stretched too far, and they because they are deprived of learning from the consequences of their unwillingness to carry their share of the load.

For an IP, Helping Is Not Extra Work

Do you find yourself annoyed when coworkers pull you away from your own assignments with requests for help, however legitimate? If so, console yourself with the thought that helping others within limits is an important part of the indispensable role you have chosen to pursue, so it is not "extra work." With this thinking, you make "mentor time" just another of the tasks to be juggled along with your other priorities.

Dottie Hepner stood at the back of the training room while the other participants in the seminar I'd conducted for a major bank paid their respects and then straggled out to their evening's activities. When we were alone, she hesitantly proceeded to tell me this sad little story.

"I'm a senior financial analyst in the bonds department, and I was recently named by my boss to a really important task force. We're to come up with some answers about an international investments program that has had problems for years. Well, two weeks ago, who should walk into one of our meetings but John Biner himself, our CEO; he sat down and asked where our thinking was going. He glanced in the folder he was carrying—I guess to make sure of my name; there were two women in the group—and said, 'Are you Dottie? What's your opinion?' Well, I don't usually have problems letting other people know what I think, but at that second my mind went blank, my throat closed up, so even if I'd thought of what to say, I don't think I could have. All I could do was just look through stuff in my folder. It was excruciating.

"Then I suppose I got saved, by Crystal Acuff, who has a job like mine in equities. 'John,' she said, 'what we've come up with thus far is that for this program to really go anywhere, we need a better policy statement from you.' Well, Mr. Biner stared at her for a few seconds, and said, 'Didn't George [the CFO] tell you that I wanted this program turned around and really profitable in three years?' 'Yeah,' Crystal shot right back at him, 'but we need to know more about what long-term effects you're looking for, what risks you're willing to take . . .'

Then Mr. Biner cut in and said, 'I'll set up a meeting with George and you five, and we'll come up with a policy. Anything else you want to ask me? Or tell me?'

"What I want to know, Dr. Bramson, is why I sat there like a ninny. I knew everything Crystal did; in fact, I was the one to realize that we needed to know a lot more before we could go ahead with planning. But you can be sure that when the investments division needs a new director, it won't be me who gets the nod."

Why should a competent, well-positioned professional like Dottie Hepner feel abashed in the presence of the rather pleasant middle-aged man I knew John Biner to be, just because he happens to be the CEO? Her reaction certainly didn't make rational sense; her friend Crystal's matter-of-fact dealings with him demonstrated that there was really nothing to fear from Biner. No wonder she felt more than a little puzzled and so down on herself that she had been so incapacitated.

Reactions like Dottie's are far from uncommon, and less extreme effects from differences in organizational rank are plainly evident. For example, notice what happens when a first-line supervisor converses with a division general manager—the way they stand, the tilt of their heads, freedom to interrupt on the part of one but not the other, the intent concentration of the subordinate, and the expression of either patient tolerance or polite indifference of the other. True, as differences in rank become smaller, the status signs become less noticeable. However, when we have played the game of guessing who is the boss in a group of strangers having dinner or playing golf, we've seldom been wrong.

Status derives from a multiplicity of differences: in rank, in wealth, and in celebrity, to name a few. It is buttressed by informal "rules" that suggest how people of more or less status should relate. Although customs have changed considerably in recent years and there is more surface informality, it doesn't take a discerning genius to detect a difference in assumed value when a subordinate shows up at an executive's door with, "I know you're very busy, but can I have just a moment of your time?" Status is alive and too well in most organizations. It's not just a concern because differences in status erode the egalitarian tone that we believe ought to be the norm. They also stifle openness in conversation and thus deprive senior managers of the perspectives and experiences of their employees; managers unknowingly allow themselves to be insulated from much of what is actually happening.

What Status Differences Do to Us

As with much else in organizational life, the varying effects of status differences on both parties rise out of a complex and interlocking set of forces.

Deference Is Enjoyed by the Exalted

The trappings and privileges of power have an ancient lineage, not only because they feed the egos of the powerful, but because they were also functional. Sounding trumpets and court etiquette supported the comforting notion that leaders were powerful—even godlike—and therefore well able to guide and protect their followers. We sometimes forget that feudal barons not only oppressed their underlings, but also protected them.

Although we may no longer deify our leaders, we do memorialize their power and prestige with elaborate offices suites, and knight them with high-sounding titles—chief executive officer rolls so nicely off the tongue—to signal their superiority, both to themselves and to those of us who serve. Unfortunately, those anointed ones seldom credit the role of sheer luck in their advancement. One of us (Robert Bramson) has sat with corporate boards as they puzzled over which of several candidates should become the next chief executive officer. Was the one chosen clearly superior to the others? Seldom so. He or she was usually the candidate whose particular attributes met some current need—often to remedy the excesses of his or her immediate predecessor—and if the directors had made their selection six months earlier or later, they probably would have chosen another of the candidates. Nevertheless, ignorant of all this and now confirmed in her belief that she is indeed special, the new CEO can secretly relish the deference paid her new role. (Of course, there is also some reality behind the assumption of executive superiority. Few executives are not in some way quite able. However, that's not the same as saying they are the *most* able.)

We See People as More Powerful than They Are

As usual, it takes two to engage in a dance like this. An accumulation of evidence suggests that we all tend to attribute to those of higher rank more power and influence than they have, and certainly more than they believe they have. We expect more of them than they are realistically capable of producing, credit their power for results that are more attributable to luck, and feel betrayed when they don't produce the miracles of which we assume they are capable. These distorted perceptions of them, together with their inflated views of themselves, prevent our seeing that they are as fallible as we are.

Status Differences Bring Out the Child in Us

Finally, deep inside each of us are memories of what it was like to be a child seeking the love and approval of parents, older siblings, teachers, and other important grown-ups. When we succeeded in pleasing them, we were praised and comforted; we felt happy and secure. When we somehow disappointed them, we were denied the approbation we desperately wanted (anything children want, they want desperately). Although we are less than fully aware of it, those old feelings can be pulled from us when properly cued by others who act toward us in some way that reminds us of our own parenting. At that moment it is not we, the strong, competent adults, who are in charge, but the weak and anxious children we once were, wishing as desperately as ever for the approval we never got enough of long ago.

Are They Really Larger than Life?

If, like Dottie, you are awed by highly placed people, make it a point to look for evidence that they are, as Crystal insisted, just like everyone else.

When I asked Dottie to try to recall the earliest time in which she remembered feeling as she did when confronted by John Biner, she slumped back in her chair, eyes closed, immobile, her expression blank. Suddenly she straightened up, eyes wide, a slight smile. "Mr. Jacobs—my second-grade teacher, Mr. Jacobs. Every time he'd call on me and I didn't know the answer, but, oh, how I wanted to. I wanted to be the best student in the whole second-grade class." She hesitated. "Biner doesn't look anything like old Mr. Jacobs—well, maybe he wasn't so old—and I did know the answer to Biner's question. And anyway, if we all have these childish feelings, how come Crystal was able to talk to him just like he was anybody? Does that mean I'm always going to be a boob with higher-ups?"

"Well," I ventured, "it's certainly true that some people are more immune to the effects of status differences than others, and if you try to talk to them about it, you'll find they have trouble even understanding what the problem is."

"You're sure right about that," she grinned. "I tried to talk to Crystal about it, and all she could say was, 'Heck, John's no different than anybody else.'"

I started in again. "Well, you could try a short spell of psychotherapy to sort out some of those leftover feelings, but short of that, there's a lot you can do to desensitize yourself so you'll feel more at ease with high-status people."

The example above points out one weakness of an otherwise very competent person. To find the "leveling" point you need to feel more comfortable with a higher-up, take some time to talk with others who know him or her and to observe that higher-up in situations where he or she might not seem so intimidating.

I asked Dottie if she had ever seen John Biner speak before an audience. She had, in fact, heard him deliver a "state of the corporation" speech before an investment community crowd. "And how did he do?" I asked.

"He was awful," she acknowledged with a grin. He had hesitated, lost his place in his notes, and looked immensely relieved when he was through.

"Yeah," I said, "John has a lot going for him, speaking well in front of an audience not included. Not only that, but based upon the presentations you made at our workshop, you're a much better speaker than he is. Isn't that right?"

"Well, sure," she said, thoughtfully.

"How about this," I suggested. "Next time you run into John, try to conjure up a picture of him faltering his way through that speech—not out of disrespect for his accomplishments, but to disabuse you of the notion that he is somehow more than just an accomplished, and very fortunate, human being."

If You Are Taken by Surprise

Many executives believe—and they are largely correct—that everything they hear from others has been carefully shaped to wrest their approval or mute their displeasure. It's understandable that they feel impelled to somehow find out "what's really going on." Not only do they range several organizational layers down to make their queries, but without necessarily intending to be rude, they sometimes sound abrupt and challenging when asking about the state of something that has caught their interest. (Very infrequently, you'll have to deal with an executive who is also of a bullying nature. For suggestions on dealing with that kind of difficult person, you might want to consult the book *Coping with Difficult Bosses*, listed in the References.)

The combination of your surprise, the executive's abruptness, and even a modicum of status anxiety can put you off stride. Clearly, what you need in your repertoire are some handy, well-rehearsed, tip-of-the-tongue phrases that will buy you a few seconds to gather your thoughts and remind yourself that this person—while powerful—is as fallible as you. Here are a few examples to start you off:

- "Just a second while I check my notes. I want to get it right."

- "What information do you already have?"

- "Could you say more about what's on your mind?"

- "That's an important question, and I don't want to give you a slipshod answer. I'll get back to you in a few minutes [a half an hour, tomorrow]."

- When you are aware that you have been silent for what seems like a long time—even though it probably hasn't been: "That's not an easy question; I'm thinking about the best way to speak to it."

Script a Heroic Role for Yourself

One way to bypass any early programming of the kind that turned financial wizard Dottie Hepner into an unsure child is to consciously imagine how you would act and sound if you related to bigwigs as the competent adult you are. Identify a friend or colleague who seems to behave naturally in dealings with those on high, and observe what he does and doesn't do—how he sounds, his posture, and anything else about him. Write mini-scripts and rehearse them out loud. Try out your role, words and all, in front of the mirror so that you can check your body language. To still any inner voices whispering that this sort of foolishness is ridiculous, remind yourself that to counter early imprinting, you need all the help you can get.

Mentally Rehearse Planned Encounters

Mental rehearsal is a well-tested method for alleviating both the anticipatory nervousness and the clumsiness that sometimes accompany learning any new skill. The technique has a double ancestry. Psychologists have been very successful in desensitizing people to rather common fears—of snakes, spiders, and high places, for example—by asking them, while safely ensconced in a cozy and supportive atmosphere, to repetitively imagine just the circumstances that they fear. Mental rehearsal has also proved itself valuable in enhancing the performance of professional and amateur athletes and others who need to learn or refine any sort of complex skills. It is not a substitute for actual practice, but Charles Garfield, who has studied peak performers in sports, business, and science, points out that visualizing demanding encounters significantly helps to improve performance and reduce inhibiting anxiety.

The nice thing about this process is that it works whether you do it well or haphazardly. You gain some benefit by simply recalling a past interaction that didn't turn out well and then rewriting the script in your imagination. For example, in Dottie Hepner's first try at mental rehearsal, she imagined herself responding to John Biner just as her colleague Crystal had, completing the scenario with a nod of respect from Biner that left her affirmed and sure of herself. (After all, since you're rewriting the script, why not give yourself a mental pat on the back?)

However, you can gain even more by approaching your mental rehearsals more systematically. In that case you would start at the beginning by visualizing the physical setting in which a VIP interaction might occur, and then imagine yourself living through a very troubling interaction. For example, you might imagine your feelings on discovering that you were missing a page of your notes while presenting a complex proposal to the executive committee. There you are, red-faced, apologizing ineffectually while you fumble through your notes, feeling like an inept child. Then use whatever relaxation techniques you've learned— deep breathing from the diaphragm with slow exhalation, perhaps—to calm yourself, letting guilt and anxiety gradually dissipate. Next, put yourself back in the boardroom, but this time see yourself calmly alleviating the tension with a clever witticism while you move on without the notes, which you didn't need anyway, to wow them with the next stage in your presentation. If you lose your focus somewhere along the way, stop, relax a bit, and start again. Force yourself to go back over that dismal sequence with its happy ending so many times that it begins to be boring. After all, that's what desensitization is all about.

Practice Your New Role in Low-Risk Situations

When you can, practice staying tension free in low-risk but real situations. For example, if you're taking a university course from an eminent professor who obviously takes himself seriously—he introduces himself as *Professor* John Smith—experiment with your new freedom in relating to important people by calling him by his first name when you ask a question. Gaze directly at him while standing up straight and practicing other bits of your new role. Naturally, the whole thing works better if you really do see him as someone above you in status and prestige.

There are many other possibilities for low-risk practice. At an off-site meeting, strike up a conversation with a vice president of a division other than your own. At a convention or professional meeting, start a discussion with a senior manager from another organization. Breaking through the coterie of hangers-on that often surrounds such luminaries can be particularly good practice.

Practicing on prestigious people in purely social situations may not have quite the same desensitizing effect, because absent their usual props and atmosphere of power, they are less likely to project an aura that declares, "I am a person of importance to whom you should naturally defer." On the other hand, if your important people are the kind who underscore their superiority by pretending to be just one of the guys (or gals), social functions may be just the place for you to practice treating them as if they were as ordinary as they claim to be.

Mediating Disagreements

Our studies of organizational decision-making styles have led us to the troubling conclusion that decisions often are less than adequate because people do not completely explore the outcomes wanted by those concerned. Worse, such lose-lose decisions often result even when the two sides have substantial areas of agreement that could have been the basis for a more productive resolution. Although it is no panacea, skilled mediation clearly might have led to fewer stupid decisions in many situations. Mediation is not magic; it is simply an integrated collection of methods directed toward these goals:

- To make sure that both parties in a disagreement feel heard and taken seriously

- To provide a trusted and relatively objective means for the participants to lower mutual suspicions and verify what others have claimed

- To assist the parties in looking for solutions that gain as much as possible for everyone

It's easy to see why indispensable people often find themselves pulled into a mediating role. Such IP qualities as a broad-gauged perspective, a knack for both listening and speaking their minds without an accompanying bite, and colleagues' trust and confidence are essential for any mediator.

The best way to acquire a high level of skill at mediation is through a mix of formal instruction and practice under the watchful eye of a mentor. However, you can get a reputation as a masterly facilitator of conflict resolution by going into action with a few of the following tried-and-true techniques. Many books and articles have been written about how to facilitate problem-solving discussions, many excellent and most of at least some value. Here, our purpose is to mention a few of the techniques we have found useful for mediating disagreements.

Know What You Both Want

A fascinating fact has fallen out of studies of two-party negotiations: the final agreement often does not include outcomes that both parties wanted. It's one thing to accede to a compromise decision when it's the only way to provide at least some gains for either or both parties, but to settle for less of what is wanted by *both* is certainly a tribute to human folly. These missed opportunities usually have several causes:

- An incomplete or distorted understanding of why each party cares about how the disagreement is resolved—that is, what both sides are hoping to get from the discussion

- Mutual apprehensions that if the other party knows what I want, the knowledge will somehow be used against me

- A mischievous underlying assumption that the game is zero-sum, meaning a gain for one requires a loss for the other

If the discussion is to progress, you must surface as many of these dysfunctional beliefs as you can and then move on to clarify what is at stake for each party.

Take the Lead in Being Open

Nothing leads better than an example. While preaching an ingenuous approach may strengthen the hand of those who already believe in it, you are unlikely to convert the slightly paranoid. But by showing yourself willing to risk laying your cards on the table (well, most of them anyway—you want to be bold, not naive), you'll exemplify openness as the proper stance for a strong and confident person. If you are a neutral mediator, you can put others at ease by confessing your trepidations in undertaking that role and your hope that whatever else happens, you will look good. You can even invite ongoing comments about how well you're doing your job. All of this serves the goal of demonstrating that it is not risky to be open.

The best negotiator I have known was a CFO who was frequently a party to large-scale acquisitions. Early in the discussion he would lead off with such gems as, "I'm just an overeducated farm boy, so could someone explain exactly what that clause means?" He insisted he wasn't trying to fool anyone—he *was* highly educated and *had* grown up on a farm—but he had found that taking that stance seemed to put others at ease.

If you are concerned that such casual admissions of "weakness" might undercut your role as mediator, keep in mind that putting yourself one down is a strong position from which to negotiate. When you are party to the discussion yourself, take the risk of revealing why the discussion is important to you, and which kinds of decisions would help you meet your goals. Make the point clear by concluding, "We need to have out on the table what each of us wants, if we're to come up with answers that will be the best for our whole organization (our community, the electric service industry, etc.)." End by directly asking a member of the group, one who has opposing interests, to be forthcoming: "How about you, John?"

Question Zero-Sum Thinking

It is difficult to arrive at the best possible resolution when both parties assume that one's gain is the other's loss. It's true that decisions often appear to bear out that assumption, but often the type of outcome is an artifact of the way the questions are posed. For example, a decision about allocating a fixed resource (a frequent cause of organizational conflict) can be taken as a perfect instance of a zero-sum problem. (If we have ten widgets and you take seven, I can only have three.) Yet ingenious solutions can develop when the competing parties give up their "I win, you lose" mentality. In one case, managers finally resolved a monthlong battle over how to make best use of a windfall of salary savings by agreeing on a trade. One department funded two positions with this year's savings, while the other had first call on an expected increase in next year's personnel budget. As in this case, most decision situations include many ways to win.

When you find yourself in a zero-sum thinking mode—"I win, you lose," or vice versa—it is important to stop the interaction by *naming* what is happening. For example, "Bob, I'm aware that this discussion is not getting us what we each need. Let's back off for a minute and see if there is a way we can each get at least some of what we want." By stopping the interaction, this naming approach often leads to a breakthrough.

Surface Underlying Issues

Polarized discussions are often manifestations of underlying issues that are too sensitive or vague to discuss openly. Until those sore points are at least acknowledged, they will block serious discussion of vital issues.

I once acted as consultant to a diverse citizens' group that was to determine the future of an aging but venerable community hospital. The hospital had once been the premier facility in a thriving neighborhood, but in recent years both had fallen on hard times. Now a fine new research-oriented teaching hospital was attracting the most prestigious physicians in the area, taking with them the upper-middle-class and well-to-do patients who had formerly been a mainstay at Community. Clearly, the community hospital's identity was at stake, but the citizens' group was not addressing these issues basic to its survival. Instead, the discussion had polarized, one faction pressing for better emergency services, and another insisting on the need to become competitive by making sizable investments in expensive but prestigious research programs.

I interrupted the discussion to ask whether the underlying issue was "Do we really want to become the poor folks' hospital?" My question evoked a bit of nervous laughter, a few whispers of "Yes, that's the question," and a chorus of relieved sighs from those who had retreated from rancorous arguments that were going nowhere. A physician who was highly thought of—he had remained loyal to a facility he obviously cared about—stood and hesitantly started to formulate his answer to that question, and then the group was able to come to grips with what was really the life-or-death issue for the hospital.

The group's decision was creative and proved to be sound. Community Medical Center now serves its less advantaged neighbors with extensive outpatient and emergency services, but it has also developed clinics and inpatient facilities unavailable at any other nearby hospital, to meet a panoply of specialized medical needs. If people don't seem to have any common ground, start hunting for unspoken issues.

Move Beyond Argument

Arguments are characterized by a repetitive lyric, the not too mellifluous drone of patronizingly delivered logic, the staccato of frequent interruption, and the wail of rising—if carefully contained—tempers. It's a familiar dirge that consistently prevents the reaching of a mutually satisfactory agreement. The basic form of the lyric is a duet in which I tell you why my alternative is the best one and why your alternative won't work. Then you reprise the theme to the opposite effect. Naturally, I never acknowledge the validity of any of your points, and you stay in harmony by never acceding to any bits of reality that I might have put forth. In its simplest form it goes something like this:

ME: I ought to have the larger office with the window because I frequently meet with important customers, and having a nice atmosphere is important to the sale. You, on the other hand, spend all your time working on your computer, so the size of *your* office and whether or not you have a window isn't important.

YOU: Now, wait a minute. I spend so much time in my office that if I were forced into that tiny space with no window, I wouldn't be nearly as productive. You, on the other hand, can meet with your customers in one of our beautiful, sound-proof conference rooms, and you don't really spend that much time in the office anyway.

After several rounds of such versifying, assuming neither of the players leaves in a huff, the level of discourse will have sunk to assertions about the truthfulness and general worth of the participants. To any listener to this duet, it's plain that the best solution is one that would benefit both sides as much as possible, and that the argumentative mode effectively prevents that.

Unfortunately, when issues need to be resolved, arguing seems to be the "default" method in the human repertoire; it obviously must have been of value to our cave-dwelling ancestors. Fortunately, as with other inherited tendencies that are no longer functional (getting physical comes to mind), when we become aware that we've fallen into a natural response that is getting in the way, we can choose something better. To reprise an earlier point, when individuals or groups are arguing, you can move them to a genuine search for the broadest-based alternative by suggesting that they are having an "either/or" kind of discussion—it might help to name it "arguing"—and then proposing a look at both the positive and the negative trade-offs that might accrue from the various alternatives.

Use Rank Ordering When Stuck

Sometimes a group has to select the best one of several generally attractive alternatives, each of which has a different mix of positive and negative attributes. A hiring decision, for instance, might involve only one opening but several likely candidates. It's not unusual for members of the group to align themselves around candidates of differing qualities, seemingly stuck because there is no one-size-fits-all alternative that would satisfy everyone.

Such deadlocks can often be broken with rank ordering. In the case of the hiring decision, group members would privately rank their top three candidates, and then the group publicly displays how many times each candidate was ranked first, second, or third. When the proponents of a particular candidate see that their first-ranked favorite was ranked second by many of those who had so vehemently argued against her, their feistiness wanes. Then the focus of discussion slowly changes from "my candidate's better than yours" to which candidate has broad enough support to be able to succeed. Often the group selects the alternative that members consistently ranked second.

Identifying and Changing a Negative Image

Most of us manage to strike a reasonably comfortable bargain with ourselves by focusing on those of our attributes we like and avoiding too close a look at those we don't. If we can't completely avoid being cognizant of our flaws, we explain them away, excuse ourselves, blame our misbehavior on others, and, in other skillful ways, sidestep the truth. Most of the time, this arrangement does little harm except, perhaps, to boost our self-esteem a little higher than is warranted.

But if you aspire to become indispensable, you're well advised to take an unvarnished look at signs that you may have acquired a trait that will take you out of the running. Here are some steps that will help you to identify whether others see you as a rather difficult person.

Check with Friends

Your friends probably know more about you than anyone else. How, then, you might wonder, can they stand being with you? The answer is that they like you, and while they really know that you are not as wonderful as you sometimes think, neither are you as reprehensible as you may imagine in moments of depression. In other words, they take you in balance, and for them, the positive outweighs the negative. That makes them an excellent source for finding out what about you bothers others.

To get useful information from friends and close associates, you'll need to give them permission to be honest. Also let them know why you're asking for their blunt perceptions: that you're bent on finally doing something about your rough edges, and it's not your intention, even if you hear starkly painful things about yourself, to end it all. Make it easier for them to downplay your annoying behavior by saying that you're interested in even the smallest, relatively insignificant aspects. Then follow up vague or general observations with requests that they be specific. Ask for examples, and look behind labels and indirect statements. For example, if your friend says that you are "usually" willing to listen, ask to know about the times when you did *not* seem to listen well. But the real key to getting honesty is this: receive any tidbits of information that are in any way negative about you with a nod of your head, a thank-you, and an enthusiastic "what else?"

Make a List

The human ability to forget unpleasantries is phenomenal. So jot down any negatives you pick up from your pals, along with what you remember of other less than complimentary comments made about you in the past. Include those stated during performance reviews, shouted by sarcastic bosses, mumbled by sullen subordinates, or quipped by jealous peers. In making your list, avoid labeling yourself as "abrasive," "seems indecisive," or "not very well organized." Instead, try to capture the specifics that others have mentioned that led them to label you in their own private thoughts.

Expect spasms of doubt that you've really done the things of which you're accused. How could this list possibly be an accurate depiction of someone as wonderful as you? Expect, too, bouts of blue funk, along with your favored symptoms of tension and anxiety. Then, after you've finished explaining to yourself or your friends that your pushiness or hot temper is entirely the fault of the stupid people who drive you to it, take a deep breath and take another look.

The point is not whether you really are everything that you've been accused of, but that you've been seen that way. You're the one who has to decide how much of what you hear is really you and how much is a function of other people's quirks, but don't let yourself slide into total denial. When you subtract the 75 percent that is due to their spleen, envy, or ulcers, you may find enough areas of agreement to convince you that *something* you're doing is turning others off.

If reading your list has made you feel like you've been hit in the face with a wet fish, you're on the right track. Your goal—painful as it might be to contemplate (and if there is no pain at all, you're doing too good a job of denial)—is acknowledging that you are not living up to your own idealized image of yourself. That done, you're ready to do the work that will minimize any annoying behaviors you've picked up that might interfere with attaining indispensable-person status.

Check It Out

If you're still not convinced that you merit a "difficult person" label, take some time to once again observe yourself in action, but this time with the specific intention of checking out whether you have indeed fallen into some of the behaviors ascribed to you. Watch yourself in meetings or while giving instructions to your subordinates. Is it true that when someone asks a question, you are always the first to answer? And is your answer pushed in the face of the questioner in that arrogantly sarcastic way that says, "How can you be so stupid?" Or do you find yourself tossing out such lukewarm pap as "You handled that reasonably well" when you know that you *should* have said, "Sally, you didn't sound prepared"? How many times during a week do you hear a derogatory edge in your voice? Ignore as irrelevant whether or not your victims deserved to be held in contempt, because that isn't the point.

The point is that if people see you as one who routinely puts others down, they won't see you as indispensable. And if some of those who feel demeaned complain, and if they are known to be valued employees, you may find yourself rated "very sharp in some ways, but we can do without him."

Paul was referred to me by his boss, the division general manager, because his "poor communication skills" were reducing the performance of his department. In a number of exit interviews, former employees had described Paul as insensitive, a "confirmed know-it-all" who frequently lost his temper and who cut down staff members regardless of their rank. Why was the company willing to pay for individual consultation for Paul? He was technically brilliant, a man of "rare scientific vision," an intense, enthusiastic whirlwind who felt personally accountable for every product that went out the door. The problem was that his department was seriously behind schedule, in part because last-minute changes ordered by Paul required substantial makeovers, and deadlines were seldom met.

As Paul's boss put it, "This guy's got so much on the ball that we'll be happy if you can break him of some of the worst things he does. For instance, stop him from rolling his eyes when someone makes a comment that he doesn't agree with. When he does that, everyone is sure that what he's thinking is 'What a jerk.' Paul works almost eighteen hours a day, every weekend, and he never takes a vacation because most of his people, including his supervisors, are angry, demoralized, and minimally productive. Paul says they're slow, but I know that they're paralyzed by the notion that no matter what they do, he's going to yell at them about it. If you can't help him, I'm going to have to let him go."

Minimize, Contain, Control

As Paul's boss implied, a *small* behavior change on your part can make the *big* difference between the perception of you as a "sharp guy with a few rough edges" and "a talented fellow, but just too abrasive (indecisive, hardheaded, shortsighted, aggressive—you fill in the blanks) to keep." Here are the steps to take when you want to manage some difficult behavior just enough so that it won't overbalance your other sterling qualities.

Limit Your Goals

Pick one or two of the behaviors from your "ugly list" that you believe might be the most irritating. One criterion might be the number of times they were mentioned by different people. Paul selected "criticizing employees in public" and "not listening" as the two handicapping behaviors that needed immediate work. True to the rule that most liabilities are exaggerations of strengths, the same quick mind and confidence that led to Paul's appointment as department head made him come across as an impatient and overly positive know-it-all.

Put on the Brakes

The instant you become aware that you're doing just what you've decided you don't want to do, stop. In practice, this means finding some socially acceptable way to break off the behavior—in midsentence, if necessary. While this is not initially easy to do, it does get easier with practice.

Select Substitute Behaviors

There are always complex reasons for behaviors like ridiculing subordinates or scolding in public, so it's handy that you don't need to fully understand what's behind your self-limiting behavior to learn to manage it better. (On the other hand, self-knowledge can help you sort out old, deeply programmed notions that limit your effectiveness and your capacity to enjoy what life has brought you, so you may want to try a bit of personal counseling also.) A good place to start is to plan what you want to do in place of the undesirable behavior.

Behaviors that you most want to stop often burst from you as if they were out of your control. So instead of enjoining yourself, "I shouldn't be that way," or even— and this is far better—"I don't *want* to be that way," think up some substitute behaviors that you can throw into the breach just after you've thrown on the brakes. Paul chose these two: "I want to hear your side of it, but let's talk about it later," and "Wait a minute; tell me more." The first he would bring into play when he realized he was publicly castigating a subordinate or accusing a peer of being stupid. The second worked well for him when he found himself interrupting or had leaped to answer a question before he knew the full story.

Soon after starting his remediation program, Paul twice found himself dressing down a subordinate supervisor during a staff meeting. The first time, he continued on with his reprimand, feeling self-conscious but unable to stop. More disturbing to him was the realization that what he had done did not stop him from starting in a second time with a different supervisor.

As Paul described it to me, "I could not believe that, having screwed up once, there I was calling Fritz on the carpet in front of everybody, doing the same damn thing again. In the past it had never even occurred to me that anything was wrong with letting people know what they've done wrong, no matter who else was

there. Still, it was better the second time. I stopped
myself in midsentence and said, 'Think about it, Fritz,'
and just moved on to the next agenda item."

Learn to Repair

It's unlikely that you will gain immediate control over
behavior patterns that have served you well—and ill—
for many years. For that reason, you'll need to repair any
damage that occurs when you slip. This can prevent the
damage from spreading and, by calling attention to your
concern for others, can help to show that you are,
indeed, a changed person. Repair has three steps:

1. Acknowledge that your behavior was not
   productive.

2. State your regret that the other person was
   discomfited by your behavior.

3. Cycle back to the circumstance that prompted
   your inappropriate behavior, this time to solve
   the problem more objectively.

Here is Paul's report of how he handled the repair
with his subordinate, Dick:

PAUL: (*sticking his head into Dick's office*) Can you
give me five minutes, Dick?

DICK: (*not looking up*) I suppose.

PAUL: (*sitting down*) What I did in the meeting this
afternoon was absolutely inappropriate. Losing
my temper is something I've done all my life, but

I know that I can't afford to do it as a manager, and I've set myself to stop, but I sure didn't that time.

DICK: You sure didn't!

PAUL: Well, if it gave you some bad moments since then, I'm really sorry.

DICK: (*slowly turning to look at Paul*) As a matter of fact, Paul, I was just sitting here thinking about trying to transfer out of the department. I don't really care what you say to me about my work, but right there in front of my own people!

PAUL: You know, it's funny, Dick, but until a little while ago, I never really thought about how losing my temper made other people feel. I guess I always thought they deserved it. Anyway, I've been thinking about what it was that set me off, and I believe it was this. I had assumed that the F38 project was about ready to go out the door, and when you mentioned that you were still fooling around with the software, I blew up. It strikes me that we need some better way to keep me up-to-date about where these projects are.

DICK: Well, you know, Paul, we still have four days to go before F38 was scheduled to be completed.

PAUL: Sure, I know that, but Del Clark has been after me about it, and from conversation I had with Joe [one of Dick's crew], I thought it was practically finished. The point is, Dick, you and I need a more regular way to review what's happening so that I don't assume all kinds of stupid things. What if we meet on Fridays from eleven to twelve to run through the project list and talk about anything else that you or I want to talk about.

DICK: Sounds like a great idea. I've been wanting to ask your advice on some personnel problems, but you always seem so busy with your own stuff that I haven't. Besides, I've told myself that I'm getting paid to solve the problems, not to bug you about them.

PAUL: And I'm getting paid to give you all the help I can. Now I'm doubly glad that we've set up these meetings.

Monitor Yourself

In Chapter 5, we reviewed some techniques for getting feedback from others. Use them, and in addition, check on how you're doing by paying close attention to others' reactions to what you say and do. For example, Paul caught the defensiveness with which Dick reiterated that the due date of his project had not yet arrived, so he was able to reemphasize that he was not further accusing Dick but was simply searching for a way to avoid similar problems in the future. Here are three monitoring questions to ask yourself:

1. How am I doing with my substitute behaviors? Am I remembering to use them? Do they need modification?

2. How well are they working? Could I be more skillful? Should I practice them in private more? Would mental rehearsal help?

3. Do others seem to react differently than before? Does she sound more, or less, defensive in our briefings? Do I still see the signs of strong emotion—red face, bouncing leg, stiffness in his body—that meant he was feeling insulted?

Review for Progress

At sensible intervals—once a week to begin with, once a month after you've seen progress—look back on how your efforts have gone. Review the specific objectives that you initially set for yourself. Have you made progress? Did you lose your temper only once last week, when in the past it was four times a week? Have you had comments from subordinates, peers, or superiors that you're easier to get along with or less moody? A pat on the back, whether delivered by an associate or by yourself, will not only make you feel good, but help you persist in your effort to rid yourself of the albatross that difficult behavior can be.

Build Support from Others

Unless there are specific reasons not to, tell your subordinates and especially your boss about your efforts to better manage your liabilities. First, that knowledge can make your colleagues ready sources of unembarrassed feedback. While monitoring yourself may be the best you can do, input from others can help you resist the temptation to explain away your slips, blame others for your outbursts, or otherwise indulge in skillful self-deceptions.

You might also be able to engage your boss as a coach. If you have a boss who is willing to observe you in action and give you clear and direct feedback, take advantage of your good fortune.

Finally, your changed behavior will more likely change perceptions about you if those who count have been alerted to what they ought to be looking for. If you have shared with your boss or your subordinates that you intend to listen better and to walk a less obviously emotional road, they will be on the lookout for signs that you are changing for the better. More than that, they will see lapses for what they are: part of any learning process and a sign that you need reminders that you still have much to learn.

8

Developing an IP Perspective

GAINING AN OWNER'S perspective, achieving a balanced life, developing a positive, can-do attitude, and learning to adjust well to change depend less upon learning new methods or techniques and more upon a redefinition of yourself as a working human being. When you act as if you were an owner, you'll find you begin to care about the health of the entire enterprise and any challenges to it. As a proactive employee, you will view every task as doable until proven otherwise. As one who adapts well to change, you will see changing circumstances as a source of new opportunity; you'll feel excited rather than uncomfortable and afraid.

If we have just described you, read no further. Apply the skills and methods outlined in Chapters 6 and 7, and you will be a cherished employee wherever you go. If, on the other hand, you are not yet there, and you've decided that becoming indispensable is for you, the exercises, suggestions, and mind stretchers in this chapter will help you to take on the perspectives that to a great extent shape the behavior of indispensable people.

Acquiring an "Owner's" Perspective

Physical exercises are strenuous activities that stretch, develop, and reshape muscles. Mental exercises do the same, except that they push you to reshape or refine the attitudes and perspectives that, over time, have become yours. Here are some exercises that can help you to encounter the events of your workdays as if you were an owner.

Cultivate a Statesmanlike Attitude

Cultivate a "statesmanlike" attitude toward turf battles and other situations that temp you to better yourself at the expense of the organization. Visualize this scenario: Marian and Todd are both members of a regional marketing team. They scrap over whose district is doing best, lobby incessantly for any promotional funds that become available, sarcastically tear down each other's ideas while pumping up their own achievements, and surreptitiously move in on each other's assigned tasks. Susan, another member of the team, stays above the fray; she patiently tries to bring the focus back to what's best for the organization, whether or not her own ideas prevail. Reality, rather than rhetoric, she implies, ought to determine who gets what, and she's willing to place her own program on the line. Not only is she *not* a "bickering child," but she shows herself to have a loftier and long-range view. In other words, she shows an owner's perspective. Who do you suppose will be seen as indispensable in this scenario? Although it may strain your credulity, it's our observation, and the opinion of every manager and executive we interviewed, that the statesmanlike Susans end up with the most resources, are chosen for the most interesting and important jobs, and are grasped tightly to corporate bosoms in every major shakeup.

There are several plausible reasons why playing the statesmanlike role has such salutary effects:

- It obviously is genuinely beneficial for the organization. In other words, one *can* do well by doing good.

- Since you will not undertake this role secretly—on the contrary, you want everyone to be quite aware of what you are doing—it creates the perception of you as a mature, "nonproblem" person who is committed to excellence. (Can you help it if others act and look childish by comparison?)

- Evidence from many studies suggests that most people are skeptical of self-praise and are far more impressed by the positive comments of others. A statesmanlike role is almost invariably noticed and discussed in private conversations, not only by superiors, but by peers (who are frequently puzzled by behavior that is not self-seeking and may be at least vaguely aware that somehow they have been one-upped, or more accurately, allowed to put themselves one down).

There is nothing perverse or unethical about playing this role. It would be hard to characterize as immoral an approach that emphasizes what is best for the larger organization, and is fair and equitable. Playing this role demonstrates a mature outlook. It would be unethical only if you were pretending this stance while secretly emulating Todd and Marian. What makes the role authentic is that in your private conversations you continue to make the case for what's good for the whole organization, letting others with more influence and power than yourself look out for your interests. That they will is a fascinating by-product.

Practice Stretching Your Field of View

As a perspective-stretching exercise, imagine yourself responsible for the success and well-being of larger and larger pieces of your organization. For example, if you are a salesperson, visualize yourself as district sales manager. What would you want to know? How would you find out? What would trouble you? Then take on the sales region, stretching yourself to visualize what that view would be like, and so on, seeing the world from the perspective of the national sales manager, the marketing and sales vice president, and finally the CEO.

Think of Yourself as a Representative at Large

When you attend a conference, convention, or seminar, think of yourself as a representative of your entire organization. Make an effort to chat with others about the problems and issues facing as large a piece of your organization as you can wrap your mind around.

Similarly, when on a trip, scan for information that might be useful to others in your organization. For example, while skimming the local newspaper, look for tidbits about local business conditions that might affect other organizational units. Are there letters to the editor that might be of use to those responsible for national marketing policies? Do remarks by local politicians point to possible regulatory changes of interest to the government agency of which you're a part?

Diagram the Potential Effects of Your Decisions

When making a decision, spend a few moments—while taking a break, for instance—to mentally diagram its effects on any other units in your organization. Let your imagination run freely. Remember that small actions can have major effects. For example, your decision to improve the quality of service *you* provide to customers may seem to bring only a slight improvement to your company, but will it provoke disappointment at a level of service previously accepted—or at least tolerated—from others in your organization? Would it be a kindness to give those others some warning that they might need to look to their service efforts?

Observe Owners in Action

Take advantage of opportunities to observe owners of successful small businesses. For example, spend your waiting time in a restaurant observing the action: who, if anyone, is monitoring quality of food and service, how they use that information, whether staff members support each other, and so forth. Think of yourself as the owner of the business. What can you see that's missing? What might be done better? How might problems be corrected?

Try to infer the owner or manager's state of mind from what she does. If possible, ask how the business is going. Listen less for particulars and more for what it's like to be an owner.

Becoming Proactive and Positively Can-Do

The genesis of a proactive, can-do outlook is, thankfully, not to be found in your genes, but in a complicated set of beliefs and odd notions that you acquired early in life, long before you could judge whether they really made sense. We know something of how a proactive perspective and its opposite develop, and it's a fascinating example of how a seemingly reasonable judgment can metamorphose into something neither expected nor wanted. At base, it works this way.

Consider the case of a hypothetical John Smith. From overheard parental remarks, "Aunt Maude was pushy as a little girl, and she's still that way," John has learned that basic human qualities don't change much over time. You are born with x amount of smarts, y amount of sociability, and z amount of aggressiveness, and that's that for the rest of your life. The neat thing about all this is that it is wonderfully self-reinforcing. As he has grown up, John has seen much that supports his belief. He's noticed, with some satisfaction, that many of his misguided acquaintances who went into therapy don't seem all that different. No wonder that he doesn't put much stock in such time wasters as employee counseling or touchy-feely management training, since such activities are all based on the notion that people can change. What John's deeply held—if erroneous—belief doesn't permit him to notice is that some of his friends seem to have benefited from therapy; he carefully explains away any change for the better as simply due to a change in their circumstances. He has even less understanding of why, when assigned a job that initially seems too much for him, he feels harassed and resentful. When he gives up on it without a real try, he either blames himself ("I just don't have what it takes") or others ("They just like to complicate everything"). John is somewhat aware that he feels most comfortable when his jobs are well within his present range of confidence.

What John is completely oblivious to—and now we're getting to the point of this tale—is that his reaction when faced with a difficult task stems from his "received" belief that, smart or dumb, aggressive or wimpy, people just don't change much. In contrast, if he had learned that people are born with somewhat stretchable minds and personalities, that they are more or less apt, depending on the situation, that they can thus be developed, then he'd be turned on by tough, demanding work, even if it seemed initially over his head. He'd relish the opportunity to stretch his abilities and be bored by tasks already within his capability.

While it's still unclear just why a can-do attitude and a belief in the mutability of human beings are connected, there is strong evidence—most of it from studies of children and young adults—that they are. If you find that you are not challenged by tough assignments, that deep inside you'd really rather stay with what you know, be of good cheer. Recognize that you didn't choose the perspectives on life that underlie those "can't-do" feelings; they happened to you. But as a thinking adult, you *can* choose to work your way toward a more proactive stance. It is absolutely possible to do that.

I have seen many others reframe notions they formerly believed to be self-evident, and I have experienced it myself. My father, a physician who labored long and hard at his profession, repeatedly lectured me on the value of mastering hard challenging tasks. But his weary demeanor at the end of each day taught me a different lesson: that one *ought* to take on tough jobs, but doing so was painful and thus to be avoided. The result for me was half a life spent sidestepping ventures that I desperately wanted to undertake. Then, with a little help from a friend, I discovered that my notion that work was always painful was as full of nonsense as a number of my other previously unquestioned beliefs.

A proactive, optimistic perspective can be learned if you are willing to reassess some of what you are absolutely positive is so. Here are two ways to start.

Reframe Inner Thoughts

When you run into a problem that doesn't seem to have a ready solution, try to identify beliefs that set you up to give up on yourself: "If I'm not quick-minded, I'm not smart," or "I lack stick-to-itiveness." Pay attention to those quick-as-a-flash thoughts that may zip through your mind; they are sometimes called "automatic thoughts" because they repeatedly follow certain kinds of negative experiences. Automatic thoughts invariably seem completely unimpeachable—the way I am—when, in fact, they were simply learned from parental criticisms, skillful teasing by older siblings, or a misanthropic teacher's subtle put-downs.

Much experience shows that when you become conscious of these mostly irrational beliefs, you can lessen their hold on you by testing them against the full reality of your experience as the rational adult you are. You can ask yourself what your experience tells you about the true level of your ability. Are you really as dumb as you were ten years ago, or have you in the interval actually learned a few things? Expect to feel a mild anxiety as you question these "truths," but keep at it. You may find that you'll do better and stay with it longer if you work with a coach. While a friend, spouse, or partner can play this role, many find that the objectivity of a counselor helps to tease out the sense from the nonsense. Other sources of help are books, including *Learned Optimism* by Martin Seligman.

When Stumped, Take a Step

When you are faced with a task that seems insurmountable, step back and look for something—anything—you can do, given your present resources. Remind yourself that a small step in any direction will often open up avenues that were not visible to you until you took that initial step. After each step, reconsider whether from this new vantage point you might now see how another step would be possible. As you continue along this path, you may find that your original pessimistic view has changed, at least a little bit.

Adjusting Well to Change

It's true: some people not only don't mind change, they relish it. Their problem, if it is one, is dashing impatiently ahead when a little steady-as-you-go would work just as well. If you're one of those, this section is not for you—although reading through it may help you to better counsel demoralized coworkers whose work world has abruptly shifted. What follows are some thoughts on the virtues of cultivating a more resilient turn of mind.

Resilience, according to the *American Heritage Dictionary*, is the ability to recover quickly from illness, change, or misfortune. Indispensable people have a lot of it, and in these days of too rapid change, we all need as much as we can get. Personal resilience has several underpinnings:

- Confidence that you will be able to stay afloat in the stormiest of seas.

- Courage to acknowledge that you have little control over anything but your own behavior. Technological fits and starts, the ebb and flow of the global marketplace, and the eccentricities of your assorted powers that be will—like the weather—be as they will be.

"The only consistent thing in my life, Doc, is change," said my client.

"And is that a problem for you?" I asked.

"Hell, no," he said with a grin. "I get a buzz out of it, but it sure seems to be a problem for a lot of my people. It's not just the changes that have happened; it's all this speculation about what else might be coming along. I keep telling them to just relax and roll with it, but just about every day I've got someone in here complaining because we're trying out some new organizational gimmick, or the compensation packages change, or the whole portfolio has to be redone because product development has come up with some new gimmick. My problem is that I just don't understand why they get so freaked out. Why can't they just go with the flow like I do?"

- Willingness to force a look at the opportunities turned up by a potentially upsetting change.

- Sense of humor. You constantly realize that you should take your work seriously, but never yourself.

These four sources of resilience draw strength from and reinforce each other. Your confidence in your own craftsmanship will ease the unpleasantness of accepting the truth that your organization will change in whatever ways will benefit it, whether or not it benefits you. As you stare down that rather bleak reality, you may redouble your efforts to add to your repertoire of indispensability skills, thus enhancing your confidence that no matter how drastic the change, it will bring opportunity for you. All of this is lightened by your realization that almost every human endeavor has a comical edge, if only you can find it.

Develop Confidence in Your Ability to Cope

It's very possible to have high self-esteem, that is, to think well of yourself, and yet not be very estimable in the eyes of others. But confidence that you can cope, regardless of what the future brings, must be grounded in both a reasonable depth of technical knowledge and a broad-based repertoire of skills that you can enhance as needed. Both require a commitment to continuous learning, one of the universal attributes of indispensable people.

Acquire Degrees, Certificates, and Diplomas

Your familiarity with the concepts, methods, and jargon of a broad range of fields allows you to keep your balance when restructurings overtake you. However, in the parallel universe of reputation, your degrees, diplomas, and certificates have an impact of their own. For one thing, they show that you are willing to persevere toward a personal objective. More important, they show you've reached a given level of competence—useful when decisions are made about who goes where at those times of rapid reshuffling that preclude a closer look.

Keep Up with Technology

As managers move up the hierarchy, they often seem to lose interest in keeping current with new technical developments. While technical matters are properly delegated to technically trained subordinates, a reasonable familiarity with new tools of the trade—especially how they might be used to understand or solve problems—will show you to be one who "keeps up." Of course, it will also strengthen your ability to effectively supervise those who report to you.

Middle managers, frequently senior in age as well as rank, often wish that their wisdom and "street smarts," hard won from years of experience, were fully appreciated by those they supervise. They are mercifully unaware that, in private conversations, their younger subordinates often dismiss them as out-of-touch relics who resist new ideas and techniques. If you are a manager, here are a few signs that you might not be staying up-to-date:

- Feeling suddenly tired or bored when a new technology is discussed

- Skipping pages when an unfamiliar area shows up in a professional article that you are reading

- Downplaying the value of a new approach because "the old way has worked well enough"

If you catch yourself indulging in any of these behaviors, pause and take stock. You may be approaching the line that divides those who are seen as keepers from those who will be cast adrift as out of touch.

Broaden Your Range of Skills

Although you might be an acknowledged subject matter expert, your resilience will depend more on acquiring the broad range of ancillary skills that characterizes indispensable people. For example, you might stretch your financial acumen by studying budget control techniques, enhance your understanding of human resources by learning how to do a job analysis or plan a training program, familiarize yourself with the basics of operating a production line, take on the task of making a deal in a foreign market, or discover how to wend your way through the complexities of a politicized government bureaucracy. Most communities have continuing education programs that provide offerings in each of these areas.

Since a major purpose of this broadening exercise is to build confidence in your ability to cope, don't take such a big bite that you end up feeling overwhelmed by all there is to learn. Instead, capitalize on what you already know. Branch out to a subject that has much in common with one you're familiar with, and then stick with it until you no longer feel lost when listening in on a conversation between experts. For example, if you are a training director, you might start your mind expansion by taking courses in employee relations and managing union contracts. As your confidence builds, extend your sights further. As you widen your range of skills, you'll feel more secure that you can function well in any circumstance and will begin to see change as the source of new opportunities rather than the loss of old.

Desensitize Yourself to Change

If you have found change troubling, and if anticipating it leaves you angry or fearful, you might benefit from two simple exercises to do when these feelings hit you: refocusing on the advantages that might result from the change, and putting yourself through a worst-case analysis in which you mentally face every horror that the change might bring. These exercises may appear too simplistic to help much, given the level of your discomfort, but they can help you past the feelings of the moment to a more objective view of the situation.

Refocus on the Positive Side of a Change

On one side of a piece of paper (or your computer screen), list several possible or probable change events that might perturb or irritate you. Try to arrange the events from the trivial—a new procedure for billing—to the traumatic—the sale of your division to a rival company (or its transfer to another state agency). To the right of each of these changes, list any possible advantages or opportunities that the change might make available to you. Force your thoughts away from any anticipated unpleasantness; you are after a reversal of perspective from the apprehensive ("It's gonna hurt") to the excited ("What goodies await me?").

Let loose both your imagination and your sense of humor. For example, here are some "advantages" that clients have dredged up once they stopped seeing themselves as victims of evildoers or an uncaring fate:

"I can finally stop worrying about being promoted to section head."

"I'll finally borrow some money and go back to school."

"It will force me to learn how to use QuickBooks. That will be a pain in the butt, but good for me."

"I'll have to move, which is all right because I don't really like my neighbors."

You'll gain from this exercise even if it merely induces you to ask the question that seldom crosses the mind of dedicated change haters: "How might this change benefit me?" But an even greater benefit, and one that can have lasting effects, will be the realization that even when you feel overpowered, you still have an important measure of control; you can determine how you will react to the change. Thus, while you may not have much to say about whether a merger will or will not take place, you *do* have control over how you will respond to it.

Although it may test your credulity when you are reeling from one change after another, what wreaks havoc on your nervous system is not stressful events in themselves, but rather a killing combination of feelings: you are angry at what's happening to you and feeling helpless to affect it. Furthermore, much evidence indicates that the way you think about how a change will affect you shapes your emotional reaction to it. The more you see change as a challenge that you can choose to meet on its own terms, the less angry and helpless you will feel, and both you and your physiological health will be the better for it.

Build a Horror Floor

One way to buttress yourself against the apprehensive feelings that often accompany an anticipated change is to engage in that gloomiest of undertakings (pun intended), a worst-case analysis. This rather reliable technique, also used to determine whether a new venture is really affordable, forces you to face the worst by mentally walking down the path of horrors. The process is simple enough; you just keep naming the worst outcome you can think of. Say, for example, that you're a senior staff member in a mental health center funded by a federal grant, and you've just heard that Congress is determined to cut the budget of your funding agency in half. Your worst-case analysis will be a dialogue something like this:

Q: What is the worst that can happen?

A: We'll have to rejustify our grant in competition with all the other mental health centers in the West.

Q: And then what's the worst that can happen?

A: We won't get funded.

Q: And then what's the worst that can happen?

A: We'll have to search for funds from other sources, and that will be a lot of work.

Q: And what's the worst that can happen?

A: We won't find any funding.

Q: And then what's the worst that can happen?

A: I'll be out of a job.

Q: And then what's the worst that can happen?

A: We'd have to live on my spouse's pay and my unemployment insurance until I find another job.

Almost invariably, when I have worked my clients through one of these awful scenarios, they have reported feeling reduced tension and renewed energy to face whatever might come. At times, especially when that final imagined event seemed to tap into a deeper fear ("Without a degree, I'd never get as good a job as I have here"), my insistent "And then what would happen?" would evoke a slow smile and an optimistically resilient reply such as "I'll be able to get back to working with my hands and not be wasting my life doing paperwork and attending meetings."

After all, the only bedrock security possible in this uncertain world is a conviction that no matter what happens, somehow, somewhere, you can find a way to live a meaningful life.

Find the Humorous Side

Every event in life has a comical aspect, even though the humor in it often escapes us when our own behavior is what makes it funny. The implicit humor in a pratfall may not quite compensate for your bruised rear end. Still, catching a glimpse of the comic side of your own or others' antics can take the steam out of almost any emotional escalation.

What most of us need is an easy-to-use device that helps keep things in perspective when that's exactly what we've lost. For example, one of us (Robert Bramson) has many times been able to stop himself from stewing over a particularly awful day by remembering an injunction by a former partner: never forget the denominator when life is rubbing your nose in the numerator. A hellish day at work won't feel quite as bad if you recall that even the worst day is only $1/365$ of a year, or $1/3,650$ of a decade, or $1/29,200$ of an eighty-year life.

Another such device is the pain scale (adapted from Tom Miller's book, *The Unfair Advantage*). Imagine a scale that ranges from 1 to 100. The score of 100 represents an excruciatingly painful event such as the total distress you would feel in losing both arms and legs in an accident. The score of 1 represents the least pain you might feel from injury that is still notice-able—a mosquito bite that is a trifle itchy, for exam-ple. At a score of 75, you might place losing one arm and one leg, and at 50 one or the other. From that frame of reference, a score of 25 would equal a three-inch cut, let's say, that leaves your arm open to the bone, 20 marks a clean stab wound in the shoulder, and 15 a thoroughly abraded knee from a hard spill. Now we're down to a score of 10 for a painful boil where you sit, and maybe 5 for a half-inch-deep cut on your forefinger from a too vigorously employed steak knife. Still left to be inserted somewhere on the scale from 5 to 1 are two very itchy mosquito bites, a bee sting (assuming you're not allergic to bee venom), and a slightly skinned knuckle. (Of course, the details of your own pain scale would depend upon any painful incidents you've experienced or witnessed, and your secret fears.)

Having gone through all the work of preparing this rating of morbid to minuscule horrors, you might as well commit it to memory. (If you've written it out, you will find it surprisingly hard to forget.)

The final step is the fun part. When you are hit by an unwelcome change and feel your usual rush of anger, frustration, or dismay, pause for a moment to decide which of the amusements on your pain scale you would be willing to substitute for that awful event. Imagine, for example, that you are employed in the central office of a small company located on the West Coast, that you have just heard your company was acquired by a larger East Coast competitor, and that at least the central office staff will be asked to move to corporate headquarters 3,000 miles away. Not only do you feel angry and frustrated, but you feel powerless to do much about it. You can, however, ask yourself, "What on my pain scale is the equivalent of this distressing change?" Would you be willing to sacrifice both arms if only you didn't have to move? No? How about one arm, or even a leg? Still no? Then would you opt for a simple, clean stab wound in the shoulder just to stay put? How about a painfully abraded knee?

Wherever you rate this event on your pain scale, thinking of it in this ludicrous way will put it in perspective—a choice between two disrupting alternatives, but not the end of the world. Yes, a decision about whether to stick with your job or to look elsewhere will never be easy; you will have to balance present costs against future benefits. But you'll face those decisions with a clearer mind and higher spirits if you can avoid what rational-emotive therapist Albert Ellis calls "awfulizing," the predilection (very hard to resist, at times) for reacting as though a crisis were a "terrible, awful, and beyond standing" catastrophe. Strange as the notion may seem, that is exactly what a pain scale can help you do.

I have talked more about how to achieve a balanced life with indispensable people than with any of my other hurried and harried clients. My guess is that a mind-set broad enough to encompass so many indispensability qualities must lead one inexorably to a realization that work is only one, albeit vital, aspect of life. When clients have asked, I have tried to share what I have seen in twenty-five years of helping dedicated people struggle to achieve a mix that was right for them. Having heard me out, most of my listeners have been at first disheartened at the complexities in what had previously seemed a straightforward, if not always easy, task, but also relieved that they were not alone in trying for an evenness of life that seemed always just out of reach. However, an unvarnished look at possibilities and problems left them even more determined to try for lives in balance. Here is the substance of what I've learned about keeping balanced in a constantly shifting world.

Toward a Balanced Life

Although everyone talks about "achieving a balanced life," no one seems able to do it for more than a day at a time. But *balanced life* is a misnomer because it implies a state of being. Balance is not a static endpoint of a process; it is a continuous process itself, requiring intervention each time it goes out of whack. Perhaps this year you sought to redress an imbalance between career and family. Next year, you may realize you haven't taken time for your favorite hobby in six months. You tipped so hard toward your family that you lost the balance between what you owe your family and what you owe your own private self.

Balancing the competing areas of your life turns out to be very much like walking a tightrope. If you lean too far one way—say, by lavishing most of your time, energy, and commitment on your career—you'll feel out of kilter and are likely to throw yourself too energetically the other way. Don't panic. Regain your balance by leaning a bit toward that aspect of your life you've slighted.

Unfortunately, you'll seldom have just one tightrope on which you must stay balanced, but a myriad among which you must often skip as the circumstances of your life change. Along with balancing career versus home life, you can expect to need a balance between high pay right now versus learning for the future, time with spouse versus time with children, busy time versus quiet time, and so on. Even if you enjoy a day, a month, or a year when all of your competing needs are in total equilibrium, any major event—a promotion, a move to another city, a new baby—will start the tightrope swinging again. Then, too, at different stages of our lives, we weigh the same things differently. What seemed trivial at thirty—long-term health needs, say—may seem vitally important at fifty. Therefore, the only time that you'll know whether your life has been well balanced—that is, you've devoted proper attention to all that has been important to you—is when you're about to leave it, and then you probably won't care much.

Rather than trying to wrest an impossible state of continuing equilibrium from a life that will stubbornly refuse to give it to you, you need to acquire the bits of knowledge and tricks of the trade that can keep you from swinging too far in one direction or another. Here are some suggestions for doing just that:

- Vital areas of your life that are starved often whimper quietly instead of shouting for help. So, when you begin to feel uneasy, look for an imbalance in the life areas most important to you.

- To keep from feeling overwhelmed when several of your "tightropes" are swinging at once, list ten answers to the question, What would most relieve my feelings of being stretched too far? Rank the items in your list from most to least attractive, and take some action on no more than the first three items.

- Make incremental changes. They are less likely to throw you off balance than a major overhaul of your lifestyle. Use a small-wins strategy whenever possible. (Refer to Chapter 6 for specific steps to take.)

- Lowering your personal standards can erode the solid center of your values and thus reduce your ability to decide what is really important to you. Follow your conscience. Ignoring its guidance will unravel the strands of all of your tightropes at once.

- When it seems as if you need to pay more time and attention to your family or yourself in order to redress an imbalance, the most practical solution is to use your work calendar to schedule time with whoever needs it most. Writing "family" in your calendar from 3:00 P.M. to 5:00 P.M. on Friday and on one or both weekend days increases the probability that you will indeed spend more time with them. Yes, of course, work exigencies and even family emergencies will erode some of that time, but, as we and many out-of-balance people can attest, building any area of your life that needs more attention into your work schedule will ensure a better balance than fervent avowals that "I need to spend more time with my family."

- Long days and weekends devoted to work are not always a sign that you're losing control over your life. The key question is, What is pushing you? If the work itself fascinates you, staying with the flow of creativity until you've reached a reasonable stopping place may be necessary for your own internal stability. If this picture fits you, you can still keep your life in balance if you openly acknowledge the extent to which your work is one of your loves, and then commit yourself to staying within some guidelines to help you keep your passion under control. For example, you might agree to give the highest priority to your kids' appearances in school concerts or plays, to stop work on Saturdays no later than 3:00 P.M., no matter what, and so forth. You will also commit to doing whatever is necessary—coffee, say, or a brief bout of exercise—that will enable you to rejoin your family circle not wearily overtaxed, but fully present and nice to have around. It's not always easy, but it can be done.

- If you're laboring long to please others or because you believe that only exhaustion can excuse anything short of perfection, you may be in danger of staying perpetually out of balance. Review the suggestions for attitude adjustment in the preceding chapters, and move time for yourself or your family to the highest priority.

When I started on this venture, I was skeptical that *indispensable* was a word that could be applied to any but a very few flaming geniuses. I was wrong, very wrong, because geniuses—seldom pleasant to have around—are often dispensed with, and true "indispensables" are often less than charismatic. In fact, it was only after discovering what they were like that I realized I had encountered and worked with more than a few indispensable people in my own consulting career—and had helped some of them become that way. The best part has been the realization that, at least to a considerable extent, any of their essential qualities could be learned by anyone of reasonable intelligence and the desire to become indispensable. If that includes you, good luck and best wishes for an exciting journey.

References

Bramson, Robert M. *Coping with Difficult Bosses.* New York: Simon & Schuster, 1992.

———. *Decision-Making Styles in Business and Industry*, Research Project No. 4845-01. Palo Alto, CA: Electric Power Research Institute, 1996.

Fromm, Erich. *Man for Himself.* New York: Henry Holt & Co., 1990.

Garfield, Charles. *Peak Performers.* New York: William Morrow, 1986.

Halpern, Diane F. *Thought and Knowledge: An Introduction to Critical Thinking*, 3rd ed. Mahwah, NJ: Erlbaum, 1996.

Harrison, Allen F., and Robert Bramson. *The Art of Thinking.* New York: Berkley Books, 1984.

InQ Educational Materials. 74 New Montgomery St., Suite 230, San Francisco, CA 94105-3411 (800-338-2462). (Information on thinking styles, their measurement, and their use for self improvement, training, and team building.)

Langer, Ellen J. *Mindfulness.* Reading, MA: Addison-Wesley, 1989.

Lebovics, Herman. "My Rose Mission." *The Wilson Quarterly* 21, 1997, p. 85. (Cites a personal communication from André Malraux to Roger Stephanie.)

Lombardo, Michael. "How Do Leaders Get to Lead?" *Issues and Observations* (Center for Creative Leadership) 2(1), 1982.

Miller, Tom. *The Unfair Advantage*. Manlius, NY: Unfair Advantage Corp., 1986.

Scott, K., K. Moore, and M. Miceli. *Human Relations* 50, 1997, pp. 287–314.

Seligman, Martin. *Learned Optimism*. New York: Knopf, 1991.

Simonton, Dean Keith. *Greatness: Who Makes History and Why*. New York: Guilford Press, 1994.

Sternberg, Robert J. *Intelligence Applied: Understanding and Increasing Your Intellectual Skills*. Orlando, FL: Harcourt Brace Jovanovich, 1986.

Sternberg, Robert J., B. E. Conway, J. L. Ketron, and M. Berstein. "People's Perceptions of Intelligences." *Journal of Personality and Social Psychology* 41, 1981, pp. 37–55.

5/on ① 15,on
5/on ④ 5/05